Practical Tools for Emotional Well-being:

Navigating Depression, Easing Anxiety, and Cultivating Mental Health

by

Sherrie R. Sall

Copyright © 2023 [Sherrie R. Salls]

Disclaimer

The information provided in this book is for general purposes only. While every effort has been made to ensure the accuracy and completeness of the content, the author makes no representations or warranties, express or implied, regarding the suitability, applicability, or completeness of the information provided. The author shall not be responsible or liable for any loss, damage, or injury that may arise from the use or misuse of the information contained in this book.

About the Author

In addition to being a doctorate-holding therapist, Sherrie R. Salls is a kind person dedicated to promoting holistic wellbeing. Although she studied human emotions extensively in her academic career, it is her ability to combine professional knowledge with real empathy that really makes her stand out.

Sherrie works to dispel stigmas associated with mental health outside of the therapy setting. She is a persistent advocate for fostering an environment of open communication and the person to turn to for workshops and heart-to-heart conversations.

Table Of Contents

11

Introduction

In the hustle of our daily lives, where emotions can sometimes feel like a maze, this book serves as a roadmap—a guide to practical tools that can illuminate your journey. Imagine these tools as keys, unlocking doors to self-awareness, resilience, and a deeper understanding of your emotional landscape.

As you explore the chapters, think of them as milestones on your personal quest for emotional well-being. Whether you're looking for ways to manage stress, navigate transitions, or enhance your relationships, each tool is a valuable asset in your emotional toolkit.

This isn't just advice; it's a conversation, a gentle nudge to empower you to take charge of your emotional health. Let these pages be a sanctuary where you can find insights, strategies, and, most importantly, actionable steps toward a more balanced and fulfilling life.

For therapists and caregivers, discover tips to enrich your support for those you guide through their emotional landscapes. Remember, these tools aren't just words on paper; they are invitations to action, catalysts for positive change, and companions on your journey to lasting emotional well-being.

So, let's embark on this exploration together. Turn the pages, absorb the wisdom, and let the practical tools within become the compass guiding you toward a more vibrant and resilient emotional existence. Your emotional well-being is a journey, and this book is here to light your way.

How to Use the Tools in This Book

Okay, let's start and discuss how to maximize the information contained inside these pages. **See this book as a reliable companion that will accompany you on your journey to emotional well-being.***

Firstly, feel free to peruse and get a feel for what's available. ***A variety of tools are available, each with a specific purpose to assist you. It's possible that one tool speaks to you more than another, and that's fantastic. We're all unique, after all, and what suits one person may not be the ideal fit for another.**

It is not necessary for you to read this book cover in one sitting. Take it one section at a time, in fact, if possible. Every tool is similar to a small adventure that is only waiting to be discovered by you. **Thus, don't hesitate to explore and try out anything that you're interested in.

**Remember that there isn't a one-size-fits-all strategy for emotional well-being as you produce. The key is to discover what speaks to you, what makes you feel more connected to the people and things in your life, more in control, and more in tune with yourself.

Certain instruments can provide an instant "aha" moment, while others may require some practice. That's perfectly typical. **Remember, progress is what matters, not perfection.

Additionally, don't be scared to customize these tools. Feel free to express your creativity, personalize, and tweak them to fit your style.** Ultimately, this journey is about you and what feels authentically you.**

Chapter 1: Workable Strategies for Self-Control

Now that we understand the fundamental reasons why workable solutions are important, let's examine the core of our emotional toolkit in more detail. In Chapter 1, we take on the role of participants in a workshop, where we learn practical skills that serve as the foundation for effective self-regulation.

Think of self-control as the compass that leads us through emotional storms. In order to gain more self-awareness and control, we're not just talking about it in this chapter—rather, we are actively investigating ways to improve our ability to pay attention, observe more clearly, and express our feelings.

Think of this chapter as a toolbox, with a different tool for navigating emotions in each part. Being more aware of our surroundings acts as a magnifying glass, enabling us to see the nuances of our emotions. Developing our observational skills is like having a set of binoculars; it helps us see the world from a wider angle. expressing feelings? We speak with ourselves in that language, which helps us become more self-aware.

Be ready to put these skills to the test as we go through this workshop's practical challenges. It's important to apply these strategies in your daily life rather than merely comprehending the idea. Now, gather your symbolic instruments and let's begin our practical investigation of self-control. All set to put on your sleeves? Start the workshop now.

Learning to Pay Attention

Developing Attentiveness is the first station in our workshop on emotions. If self-control is the goal, then being aware of our surroundings is the road that gets us there. We're going to venture into the world of mindfulness in this section, where learning to pay attention turns into a useful skill for negotiating our emotional terrain.

Think of being attentive as a spotlight that shines on the current moment in the mental theater. It's about accepting the subtleties of your thoughts and feelings without passing judgment and living in the present moment. Imagine it as turning on the music to your life and being able to clearly hear the notes and silences.

Practically speaking, intentional, tiny actions are necessary to cultivate attentiveness. It could be as easy as taking a few minutes to concentrate on your breathing, noticing the specifics of thoughts and feelings as they come to you. This is about developing a soft awareness, not about being too vigilant.

Why is this relevant? The basis for self-awareness is attentiveness. It enables us to spot trends, pinpoint stressors, and comprehend the rise and fall of our emotional states. Consider this exploration of this feature as the refinement of a skill; the more you work at it, the more automatic it becomes.

Take this chapter as a voyage into the art of being present as you immerse yourself in it. These exercises and insights are calls to practice attentiveness in your everyday life; they are more than just concepts. Are you prepared to set out on this mindful exploration journey? Now let's start cultivating attentiveness.

Improving Observational Proficiencies

Let's highlight the next station in the emotional workshop, Improving Observation Skills, as we carry on with our investigation. Consider this as honing your radar so you can detect the minute details that mold your emotional terrain.

The detectives in our toolbox, observation skills enable us to find the cues concealed in our feelings, thoughts, and environment. The idea behind increased observation is to picture yourself strolling through a well-known park and taking note of the minute variations in the breeze, the delicate patterns on the leaves, or the way the sun plays on the grass.

This chapter encourages you to become an astute observer of your own experiences in real life. It might be as simple as writing in your journal about your day, focusing on the subtleties that are sometimes missed. Alternatively, it could entail taking a moment to intentionally stop and observe the hues, patterns, and noises surrounding you, using all of your senses.

Why does this matter? Improved observational abilities help us comprehend the world both inside and outside of ourselves. They enable us to identify trends, triggers, and happy moments that we might otherwise miss. This ability is about having a keen mind, asking questions, and looking for solutions in the little things in life.

Consider this section of the course as a trip to develop into a perceptive observer of your own life as we move forward. The exercises offered invitations to view the world in a different light rather than merely tasks. Are you ready to improve your ability to observe? Together, let's go off on this adventure.

Developing Emotional Expression

Greetings and welcome to the third station of our workshop on emotions: Enhancing Emotional Expression. If becoming more aware of your surroundings is like tuning into your emotions, then improving your observational skills is like being a sharp observer. The language that lets you communicate what you learn is called articulation.

Consider articulation to be the emotional journey's storyteller. It entails figuring out how to express the subtleties of your feelings using words, metaphors, or even pictures. This chapter explores the art of verbalizing your feelings, offering insight into the frequently enigmatic and intricate realm of emotions.

Practically speaking, talking to oneself will help you become more articulate. One way to express yourself could be by journaling, which involves putting your emotions into words. As an alternative, it could be using artistic or musical mediums to express yourself, or it could just be a straightforward chat with a reliable friend. To close the gap between how you feel and how you communicate those sentiments is the aim.

Why is this relevant? A clearer voice contributes to self-awareness. It makes it possible for you to express your emotions more clearly and to identify what you're feeling. It's similar to learning how to play the notes of your emotions.

Consider this section of the course as a journey to discover your own emotional language as you enter it. These activities are not only assignments; rather, they are calls to investigate the depth of your emotional lexicon. Are you prepared to express your feelings more clearly? Now let's explore this expressive section of our workshop on emotions.

Developing Introspection

Let's move on to the last section of our emotional training, which is Developing Self-Awareness. If becoming more alert is like tuning into your emotions, becoming more perceptive is like sharply sensing them, and becoming more articulate in like expressing them, then becoming more self-aware is the culmination of these abilities into a deep comprehension of who you are.

Think of self-awareness as the map that helps you navigate the complex emotional landscape that is you. It entails knowing why you feel the way you do in addition to just acknowledging your feelings. This chapter is an invitation to take control of your inner world and navigate the emotional waters with clarity.

Developing self-awareness practically means analyzing your emotional reactions, seeing trends, and making connections between your ideas, feelings, and behaviors. It might be checking in with yourself on a regular basis, writing in a journal about your experiences, or asking mentors or close friends for advice.

Why is this an essential component of our emotional armory? The foundation of emotional intelligence is self-awareness. It gives you the ability to make deliberate decisions, deal with obstacles more skillfully, and develop a strong sense of wellbeing.

Consider this chapter as a study of the complex terrain that is you, as you immerse yourself in it. These exercises are calls to go on a journey of self-discovery, not just tasks. All set to develop self-awareness? Now let's explore this transforming facet of our works

Chapter 2: Supporting Clients in their Journey

Being a compass for someone who is traveling through unfamiliar territory is what it means to support clients in therapy. Creating a secure area where people may delve into the depths of their emotions, anxieties, and goals is just as important as providing direction.

Helping clients is a collaboration rather than just a job. It entails being there for them through their highs and lows, offering support and guidance as they traverse their emotional terrain. As we explore tools that go along with this suggestion, remember that the most important thing is to be a helpful presence in your customers' travels. Are you prepared to use these instruments with me? Let's carry on with our therapeutic investigation using this human-centered methodology.

2a. Strategies for Active Listening

Active listening is a subtle technique that involves more than just hearing what is being said in therapy. It entails setting up an environment where your clients experience value, understanding, and hearing. Here is a thorough how-to guide for mastering this ability:

Give It Your All:

Engage in conversation both mentally and physically. Set aside all distractions, including phones and other work, and give the client your whole attention.

Keep Eye Contact:

Making eye contact is a potent nonverbal indication that indicates focus. It helps to build rapport and reassures clients that you are paying attention to what they are saying.

Make Use of Inviting and Open Body Language:

You should project warmth and openness through your body language. Sit in a posture that conveys openness and a willingness to listen, rather than crossing your arms.

Give a nod and offer affirmations:

Nodding and offering positive statements like "I see," "I understand," or "Go on" are examples of nonverbal cues that show the client you are actively listening to them and want them to share more.

Introspective Reactions:

Practice summarizing the client's words or reflecting back. This gives the client the assurance that you understand them and makes them Feel heard and valued.

Pose Inquiry-Based Questions:

Encourage your clients to share their thoughts by posing open-ended inquiries. These questions encourage more in-depth answers and give clients room to explore their emotions and ideas in greater detail.

Don't Interrupt:

Give customers time to finish expressing themselves before answering. Interrupting might throw off the rhythm and give the impression that you are impatient or unkind.

Verify Your Feelings:

Recognize and respect the client's feelings. Consider the emotional depth of their communication and show understanding and empathy.

Recap and Explain:

Recap the client's words every so often to be sure you've understood them correctly. If something doesn't seem clear, make sure it is understood.

Develop Empathy:

Consider yourself as the client's advocate. Recognize their viewpoint without passing judgment, and show empathy in your words and actions.

Don't Assume Anything:

Put away assumptions or preconceptions. Be open-minded and let the client's individual experience evolve in every session.

Engage in Mindful Hearing:

Give each moment your whole attention. Reduce the amount of time you spend thinking about your response while the client is speaking and instead concentrate on listening intently.

You may create a space that promotes trust and open communication by implementing these techniques into your therapy approach. In order to build a solid therapeutic bond and support your clients' meaningful exploration and growth, active listening becomes a fundamental component.

2b.Empowerment strategies

In therapy, empowerment techniques provide the framework that helps patients build their own paths to resilience and self-efficacy. Creating an atmosphere where clients may identify their abilities, make decisions, and find their own pathways is more important than providing answers. Here's a thorough look at using empowerment techniques in your therapeutic work:

Strengths-Based Methodology:
Determine and highlight your client's advantages. Assist them in realizing the resources and

capabilities they already have, helping them feel empowered by their own strengths.

Setting Goals Together:

Help customers define their own objectives. These objectives ought to be clear, attainable, and consistent with the client's beliefs. By working together to create goals, clients are empowered to participate actively in their journey.

Promote Autonomy:

Assist customers in reaching decisions. Motivate kids to accept accountability for their deeds, cultivating a sense of independence and accountability for the course of their life.

Examining Beliefs and Values:

Help customers define their views and values. Clients who live in accordance with their guiding values can have a greater sense of empowerment and purpose.

Exercises to Develop Skills:

Encourage your client to participate in skill-building exercises that will improve their coping strategies and problem-solving techniques. This gives kids useful tools to deal with obstacles in life.

Positive Discipline:

Celebrate and give thanks for minor wins. Encouraging feedback fosters a feeling of success and supports the notion that individuals can bring about constructive transformations in their lives.

Encouragement of Self-Reflection

Urge your clients to consider their personal perspectives and learning. Through this process, they become more self-aware and are encouraged to come up with their own solutions.

Information Provision:

Provide psychoeducation and pertinent information. Clients gain information from this and are more equipped to make decisions regarding their mental health and general wellbeing.

Building Up Resilience:

Examine techniques for enhancing resilience. Assist clients in realizing that they are resilient and that obstacles can serve as chances for personal development.

Validating Individual Agency:

Promote the idea of personal agency, or the conviction that people have the power to affect their own life. By doing this, the emphasis is shifted from outside variables to the client's inherent ability to change.

Establishing a Helpful Environment

Encourage a supportive and trusting environment. Clients may express themselves in a safe atmosphere without worrying about being judged, which gives them confidence to be real.

Promote Self-Advocacy:

Assist clients in communicating their requirements and standing up for themselves. Effectively navigating interpersonal and external systems requires this ability.

Therapists can establish a partnership with their clients in which the latter take an active role in their own development by incorporating these empowering tactics. It's about pointing the path and offering the resources, but in the end, allowing clients to create and mold their own path toward empowerment and wellbeing.

2c: Goal setting approaches

In therapy, goal-setting techniques are similar to creating a customized road map that leads patients toward significant and attainable goals. It entails working together with customers to determine attainable objectives that complement their desires. Now let's explore the subtleties of successful goal-setting in therapeutic settings:

Establishing Collaborative Objectives:
Establish goals by working together in a collaborative method. By doing this, it is made sure that clients feel empowered and take pride in the process of creating goals.

Particular and Quantifiable Goals:
Urge clients to state clear, quantifiable objectives. This clarity offers a path forward and for tangible assessment.

Connection to Values:

Link objectives to the values and ambitions of your clients. Goals gain motivation and a sense of purpose when they are consistent with underlying beliefs.

Achievable and Reasonable Goals:

Assist customers in establishing reasonable and doable goals. This encourages a sense of accomplishment and lessens emotions of overwhelm.

Time-Limited Structure:

Define a deadline for completing the task. This gives customers structure and aids in maintaining focus, which promotes a sense of dedication and urgency.

Dividing Larger Objectives:

If your clients have big objectives, break them down into more doable chunks. This facilitates incremental progress and makes the journey easier to handle.

Taking Customer Preferences Into Account:

When defining goals, take into account the preferences and preferred methods of your clientele. Adapting the procedure to each person's unique style increases dedication and involvement.

Frequent Evaluation and Modification:

Review your progress frequently and remain flexible in modifying your objectives. Setting goals that are flexible allows for the adjustment of objectives or changes in priorities.

Rejoicing in Milestones:

Recognize your progress along the way. Acknowledging advancements helps clients feel more competent and inspires them to keep working toward their objectives.

Resolving Possible Obstacles:

Consider and talk about possible obstacles to achieving your objectives. Clients who learn how to overcome difficulties are more equipped to handle challenges.

Adhering to the Therapeutic Objective:

Make sure the objectives support the client's general well being and are in line with the therapy focus. This integration encourages a comprehensive method of goal-setting.

Promoting Internal Motivation:

Examine the underlying drives that each objective has. Realizing the bigger picture strengthens dedication and encourages a feeling of personal involvement.

Setting goals in therapy is a dynamic and changing process that calls for constant cooperation and introspection. By combining these strategies, therapists enable their patients to take control of their recovery process, helping them to feel accomplished, directed, and purposeful as they move toward emotional well-being.

2d:Mindfulness Integration

Incorporating mindfulness into therapy is similar to bringing a calm breeze into the therapeutic environment because it promotes profound awareness of one's inner experiences and present-moment awareness. Let us examine the effective integration of mindfulness into therapeutic practice:

Consciously inhaling:

Spend a few minutes breathing mindfully before each session. Encourage clients to concentrate on their breathing to help them feel grounded and at ease.

Exercises for Body Scan:

Include body scan exercises to help clients investigate their sensations in various body areas in a thoughtful manner. This improves somatic awareness and strengthens the mental-physical bond.

Taking Note of Thoughts and Feelings:

Assist clients in objectively monitoring their feelings and ideas. The practice of mindfulness promotes non-reactive awareness, which makes it possible to examine inner events more objectively.

Active Listening:

During sessions, practice listening with awareness. In order to create a deeper connection and understanding, this entails listening intently to the client without pre-forming a response.

Exercises for Mindful Eating:

To improve your awareness of the sensory aspects of eating, try some mindful eating exercises. This can be especially helpful for people who struggle with eating disorders and body image concerns.

Walk With Awareness:

Encourage clients to walk mindfully if at all possible. In order to foster a sense of present and grounding, this entails paying attention to each step and the sensations connected to movement.

Methods of Mindfulness-Based Stress Reduction (MBSR):

Introduce MBSR practices including mindful body movement and guided meditation. These methods give clients useful tools for integrating mindfulness into their everyday routines.

Observant Journaling:

Encourage the practice of mindful journaling. To foster self-reflection and awareness, encourage clients to write about their thoughts and feelings.

Cognitive Therapy Based on Mindfulness (MBCT):

Include MBCT components for individuals who experience recurring anxiety or depression. In order to stop relapses, this method combines cognitive therapy with mindfulness exercises.

Developing Appreciation:

Include exercises on thankfulness in your sessions. Reminding oneself of the good things in life might help one refocus and feel better emotionally.

Using Mindfulness in Coping Mechanisms:

Instruct clients on incorporating mindfulness into their coping mechanisms. Mindfulness can be an effective approach for managing difficulties, whether stress, worry, or challenging emotions are being dealt with.

Using mindfulness when visualizing

Lead clients through visualization exercises that are focused on mindfulness. They can develop a resilient and peaceful mental environment as a result.

Therapists who skillfully incorporate mindfulness into their therapeutic practices enable their clients to become more acutely aware of the present moment. This method not only improves mental health but also gives clients useful tools to help them navigate the challenges of life more resiliently and clearly.

2e:Strengths-based counseling

A transformative approach, strengths-based therapy emphasizes and makes use of an individual's innate qualities and talents, moving the focus from disease to resilience. It's an empowering and cooperative approach that strengthens the therapeutic partnership. A closer look at the application of strengths-based therapy is provided below:

Finding and Enhancing Your Strengths:
Start by determining the client's strengths in concert with them. This could include virtues, aptitudes,

skills, or strengths of character. As the therapy session progress, emphasize these positive traits.

Optimistic Rephrasing:

Urge clients to see the bright side of obstacles and failures. Examine how they can use their strengths to overcome obstacles and come up with solutions.

Setting Goals Together:

Assist customers in creating objectives that play to their strengths. This cooperative method boosts motivation and gives therapy sessions a defined course.

Tools for Assessing Strengths:

To discover and investigate a client's special capabilities, use strengths evaluation instruments. This can include inventories that focus on strengths, such as the VIA Survey of Character Strengths.

Building a Successful Therapeutic Partnership:

Encourage a cooperative and constructive therapy relationship. Celebrate and acknowledge accomplishments while fostering a supportive and motivating environment.

Language Based on Strengths:

When interacting, speak from your strengths. Talk about the things that customers can accomplish, highlighting their skills and room for improvement.

Including the Principles of Positive Psychology:

Incorporate the concepts of positive psychology into therapy sessions. Examine subjects like thankfulness, fortitude, and the search for meaning and purpose.

Tools for Narrative Therapy:

Help clients rewrite and reconstruct their life stories with an emphasis on strengths, resilience, and personal development by using narrative therapy tools.

Interventions Based on Strengths:

Put particular strengths-based interventions into practice. This could entail exercises or activities that specifically target and strengthen recognized strengths.

Promoting Introspection:

Encourage clients to reflect on their past accomplishments and examples of perseverance. The basis for identifying and leveraging strengths is established by this introspection.

Validating and Confirming:

Verify and affirm your clients' strengths on a regular basis. This affirmation strengthens their sense of self-worth and their confidence in their capacity to overcome obstacles.

Using Strengths to Measure Progress:

Create metrics for improvement that emphasize strengths instead of just symptom reduction. This method offers a comprehensive perspective on wellbeing.

Strengths-based counseling is a worldview that recognizes each person's potential and resilience, not only a therapeutic technique. Therapists enable their clients to face obstacles with a renewed feeling of optimism and self-efficacy by highlighting and celebrating their strengths.

2f :Cultural Competence

In the field of therapy, cultural competence refer to the ability to comprehend, value, and collaborate productively with people from a variety of cultural backgrounds. It entails recognizing how culture affects clients' experiences and modifying therapy techniques to be sensitive and inclusive. The following are some tips for incorporating cultural competency into your therapeutic work:

Cultural Deference:
Develop a humble attitude toward culture. This entails realizing that cultural competency is not a collection of predetermined skills but rather a continuous process of learning and introspection.

Cultural Sensitivity and Instruction:
Keep learning about other peoples' cultures, customs, and worldviews. Remain aware of cultural

quirks that could affect a client's perspective and experiences.

Transparent Communication:

Have frank discussions about clients' cultural identities with them. Invite them to discuss how their cultural upbringing affects their beliefs, attitudes, and expectations.

Culturally Sensitive Evaluation:

Adjust evaluation procedures to reflect cultural differences. This entails understanding cultural variances in distress expressions, including cultural considerations into diagnostic criteria, and modifying assessment instruments appropriately.

Courtesy toward diversity:

Accept and value the differences between and within civilizations. Refrain from drawing conclusions based on preconceived notions and pay attention to the distinctive experiences of each person.

Linguistic proficiency:

Develop language proficiency in the languages that your clients speak, if applicable. This promotes cultural inclusion and facilitates successful communication.

Cultural Prudence:

Establish a safe space for different cultures where clients can feel appreciated and validated. This entails establishing a judgment-free environment, recognizing power dynamics, and being conscious of any potential biases.

Combining Different Cultural Practices:

When it makes sense, be willing to incorporate cultural customs and practices into therapy. This could involve using analogies that are appropriate for the culture, rituals, or ceremonies.

Setting Goals Together:

Goals for therapy should be jointly determined and should reflect the client's cultural beliefs. This guarantees that the client will find the treatments meaningful and relevant in their culture.

Being Aware of Intersectionality:

Acknowledge and comprehend intersectionality, which is the way that different social identities—like race, ethnicity, gender, and sexual orientation—are connected to one another. Examine how a client's experiences are shaped by the intersection of these aspects.

Consultation on Culture:

Consult a cultural consultant when necessary. Seek advice from professionals or associated with specialized knowledge in a certain ethnic group to improve your comprehension and proficiency.

Taking On Cultural Preconceptions:

Identify and confront cultural preconceptions and prejudices, both in the therapeutic setting and within yourself. Create a space where clients feel free to talk about their experiences without fear of repercussions.

Being culturally competent is a dynamic process that calls for constant learning and modification rather than a one-size-fits-all strategy.

Therapists can establish a more successful and inclusive therapeutic environment that respects the many experiences and backgrounds of their clients by incorporating these strategies.

2g Trauma-informed care

In therapy, trauma-informed treatment is an approach that acknowledges the pervasive effects of trauma on people and places a strong emphasis on establishing a secure and encouraging space for recovery. It encompasses the impacts of trauma, including trauma-sensitive procedures, and enabling people to reclaim their resilience and sense of control. To incorporate trauma-informed treatment into your therapeutic practice, follow these steps:

Recognizing the Frequency of Trauma: Acknowledge that trauma affects people of all backgrounds and is pervasive. Recognize the different types of trauma, such as development, interpersonal, and social traumas.

Establishing a Secure Environment: Provide a friendly and secure therapeutic atmosphere. In addition to emotional and relational safety, this also refers to physical safety, which gives clients the confidence to investigate and talk about their experiences.

Establishing Trust:

Give establishing and preserving client confidence first priority. Recognize that building trust might take some time, particularly for those who have previously been the victim of treachery or other breaches.

Language Informed by Trauma:

Make use of language that is trauma-informed and stresses choice and empowerment. Steer clear of words that could retraumatize someone or hold them accountable for their experiences.

Identifying the Causes of Trauma:

Be aware of any possible triggers for trauma. Be aware that some words, gestures, or circumstances could bring up painful memories for people who have suffered trauma.

Boosting Individuality and Choice:

Involve patients in treatment decisions to empower them. Whenever feasible, provide options while honoring their agency and sense of autonomy during the therapeutic process.

Cultural Awareness:

Cultural sensitivity should be incorporated into trauma-informed care. Be aware that a person's culture may have an impact on how they feel and communicate trauma. Recognize how trauma and culture interact.

Teaching Clients about Reactions to Trauma:

Inform clients on typical reactions to trauma. This entails recognizing and normalizing the fight, flight, freeze, or fawn emotions in relation to trauma.

Do Not Assume Anything:

Refrain from assuming anything about a client's experience just because they disclosed trauma. Since every person reacts to trauma differently, stigmatization may persist due to presumptions.

Promoting the Use of Self-Regulation Strategies:

Teach and promote self-control strategies. Teach clients how to control their emotional and physical reactions to triggers by teaching them mindfulness techniques, grounding exercises, and other techniques.

Trauma-Informed Evaluation:

Adapt assessment instruments to account for trauma. During the diagnostic process, take into account how trauma may affect replies and exercise caution in case someone gets traumatized again.

Setting Goals Together:

Together with your clients, develop trauma-informed goals. Recognize their perseverance and strengths while acknowledging the particular difficulties they could encounter while recuperating.

The continual commitment to comprehending and addressing the effects of trauma is known as trauma-informed treatment. Therapists can foster an environment that supports trauma survivors' resilience, empowerment, and recovery by incorporating these ideas into their therapeutic practices.

2h:Effective communication skills

Effective communication is the cornerstone of successful treatment because it fosters a strong therapeutic alliance and an atmosphere in which clients feel hard, understood, and supported. An overview of the primary communication skills needed for therapeutic treatment is provided below:

Paying close attention:

You can show that you are actively listening to a client by offering them your whole attention, actively engaging in their conversation, and showcasing your knowledge through both spoken and nonverbal cues.

Reflective Response:

Employ considerate responses to validate and clarify the client's assertions. Responding to their thoughts and feelings demonstrates your understanding of them and encourages more research.

Empathic Sensation:

To relate to the client's feelings, cultivate empathy. Consider yourself to be the person they are experiencing in order to acknowledge and show them how much you value their feelings.

Non-Verbal Communication:

Observe your facial expressions, gestures, and body language when engaging with other people. It is possible to convey attentiveness, empathy, and openness through nonverbal clues.

Open-ended questions:

Ask open-ended questions to elicit reflection and conversation. Clients can provide more information to the therapeutic conversation by responding to these questions.

To sum up:

At frequent intervals, summarize the key points to ensure that everyone is aware of the client's story and to ensure that everyone is on the same page. This improves your relationship with clients by assisting them in seeing patterns or connections in their experiences.

To be precise:

Clarify any remarks that are unclear or ambiguous to avoid misunderstandings. When in doubt, get further information to be sure you comprehend anything.

Cultural Intelligence in Social Contexts:

Respect and be mindful of the different cultural norms and communication styles that are out there when you communicate. Adjust your approach to accommodate for the cultural background of the client.

Collaboration in Phrases:

Communicate in a way that emphasizes teamwork throughout the therapeutic process. Phrases like "we can work on this together" encourage teamwork and shared responsibility.

Avoid making assumptions and passing judgment:

Remain objective and don't make any assumptions regarding the client's background. Provide a space where clients can speak openly without fear of criticism.

Psychoeducation:

Successfully convey psychiatric concepts and therapeutic methods. Give clients information about their mental health and the therapy procedure in an approachable and clear manner.

Remarks and Verification:

Give constructive feedback when it's appropriate and recognize the client's accomplishments. Positive feedback encourages motivation and a sense of accomplishment.

Indifferent Silent:

Allow them some time for respectful quiet. People can learn to reflect and process their thoughts and feelings more easily when there is silence.

Flexibility in Communication Style:

Adapt your communication style to the particular needs and preferences of each client. Adaptability ensures that your plan meets the unique needs of the therapeutic partnership.

By employing these communication strategies, therapists can establish a strong therapeutic alliance that will encourage genuine and insightful discussions that support clients in their pursuit of well-being.

2i Self-care Practices

For therapists to stay well and effectively help their clients, self-care is essential. Therapists can include the following self-care techniques in their daily practices:

Frequent Consultation and Supervision:
Participate in routine mentorship or supervision with coworkers. This is a helpful forum for talking about difficult cases and getting advice.

Individual Counseling:
Take part in your own treatment to deal with issues that are personal and professional. This helps you become more self-aware and improves your capacity for client empathy.

Determining Limitations:
To preserve a good work-life balance, establish clear limits in your professional life. Stir clear of working

too much overtime and make time for leisure and personal life.

Techniques for Relaxation and Mindfulness:

Engage in awareness and relaxation exercises like yoga, deep breathing, or meditation. These methods can support mental health and aid with stress management.

Frequent Workout:

Include physical activity on a regular basis in your schedule. Exercise is good for mental health in addition to its benefits for physical health.

Interests and Passive Activities:

Allocate time for interests and pastimes that make you happy and calm. This can be anything you find reviving, including reading, painting, or gardening.

Social Networks:

Develop relationships with friends, family, and coworkers on a social level. Creating a robust support system offers channels for receiving and giving support

Holidays and Downtime:

Take regular breaks and vacations to rejuvenate. It's crucial to take occasional breaks from work to avoid burnout.

Writing a Journal:

To help you reflect on your feelings and experiences, keep a notebook. Processing ideas and emotions might find a therapeutic expression in journaling.

Ongoing Instruction:

Take part in continuing education and professional development. Keeping up with the latest findings and methods can revitalize your work.

A nutritious diet:

Be mindful of your eating habits. A healthy, well-balanced diet can affect your mood and energy levels in addition to improving your general well-being.

Restful Sleep:

Give adequate sleep a priority. To guarantee that you get enough sleep, set up a regular sleep schedule and make your surroundings sleep-friendly.

Frequent Visits

Assess your emotional health by checking in with yourself on a regular basis. Identify and treat stress or burnout symptoms as soon as you notice them.

Restorative getaways:

Think about taking part in courses or therapy. These encounters may provide you with renewed energy and fresh insight into your work as a therapist.

The Creative Arts:

Investigate your creative and artistic options. Using creativity as a therapeutic outlet to release tension and express feelings can be beneficial.

Recall that taking care of yourself needs conscious effort and is a continuous process. Making time for your health matters not only helps you help clients better, but it also helps you have a long-lasting and satisfying career in therapy.

2j :Continued professional development (CPD)

Continuing professional development (CPD) is essential for therapists to keep current, enhance their skills, and provide the best care possible for their patients. The following are some methods for carrying on with your career development:

Attend workshops and conferences:

Attend workshops, conferences, and seminars related to your field of therapy. These events offer opportunities to learn from experts, explore new concepts, and network with colleagues.

Webinars and online classes:

Take part in online courses and webinars. With the aid of multiple websites offering courses on various therapeutic issues, you can study at your own pace.

Observation and Guidance:

Continue offering guidance or acting as a manager. Having regular discussions with mentors or more experienced colleagues provides sage guidance.

Look Through Academic Writings:

To keep informed, read academic books, research papers, and related periodicals on a regular basis. This keeps you up to date on the latest developments in your field.

Become a member of professional organizations:

Join professional associations in your area of expertise. These organizations usually provide information, conferences, and networking opportunities.

Seek Out Professional Guidance:

Pursue specialized training in particular fields of interest or therapeutic modalities. You can increase your area of expertise and offer a greater range of services by doing this.

Engage in Joint Supervision:

Participate in peer monitoring groups. Collaborating with fellow therapists fosters a secure setting for discussing cases and exchanging perspectives.

Follow Up on Legal and Ethical Needs:

Regularly review and stay current on the legislation and ethical standards relevant to your field of work. This ensures that your practice follows the highest standards set out by the profession.

Utilize Resources for Online Education:

Look into online learning platforms that provide classes on many therapeutic topics. Online resources like Coursera, Udemy, and LinkedIn Learning can be quite helpful.

Collaborate with Your Coworkers:

Collaborate with others on joint ventures or research endeavors. Working together can provide a variety of perspectives and opportunities for mutual learning.

Reflective Techniques:

Every day, make introspection a habit. Regularly review your own therapeutic work, highlighting any areas that want improvement.

Mentoring Programs:

Seek out mentoring programs. Having a mentor can assist you in managing your career by offering guidance, support, and sage counsel.

Possibilities for Training and Instruction:

Investigate opportunities to coach or mentor others in your field of expertise. By sharing your knowledge, you enhance your own understanding and influence the next wave of therapists.

Stay Tech-Savvy:

Keep up with any technological advancements that impact your field of work. This entails being aware of telemedicine platforms, electronic health records, and other tools that can enhance the therapeutic work you perform.

Remarks and Evaluation:

Consult with supervisors, colleagues, and clients for advice. To ensure continuous progress, evaluate your own work on a frequent basis and be open to constructive criticism.

Continued professional development is the lifetime commitment to study and career advancement. You can ensure that your practice grows, your skills remain current, and you provide the best service to your clients by continuing to engage in these activities.

Chapter 3:Techniques for Overcoming Thoughts of Depression

This chapter will look at useful techniques for navigating and overcoming the difficult terrain of depressive thoughts. Although depression can cast a dark shadow, people can start to see some bright spots if they have the correct resources. Let's explore these tactics while keeping in mind that no two people's journeys and that no one size fits all.

Knowing What Depressive Thoughts Are

Understanding the nature of depressive thoughts is essential before we go into the tools. These can include intrusive negative self-talk and enduring melancholy. Regaining control over one's mental health begins with identifying and accepting these thoughts.

3a:Journaling

Investigating the Depths of Writing
Writing in a journal is a voyage of self-discovery and emotional expression, not merely putting pen to paper. Here's how utilizing this straightforward yet deep exercise can help you navigate the complexity of sadness and become a transforming tool.

1. Setting the Scene: See your notebook as a hallowed place, a blank canvas on which your ideas and feelings are painted. Start by selecting a time that is calm, setting up a cozy space, and allowing the pages of your diary to become a safe refuge for your deepest ideas.

2. Unfiltered Expression: You are able to express yourself freely when you journal without fear of criticism. Flow onto the pages with your emotions, not worrying about consistency or accuracy. It's an honest, unvarnished conversation with yourself.

3. Capturing the Darkness: Write down the main ideas that come to mind when you're feeling down. Explain the sensation of weight, lingering shadows, and overwhelming feelings. Permit the shadows to speak through the pages.

4. Examining Triggers: Make a list of all the things that could set off your gloomy thoughts. Determine and examine them in your journal, whether they are particular events, persons, or even ideas. The first step towards comprehension is awareness.

5. Tracking Patterns: You can spot trends in your mood and cognitive patterns by keeping a journal over time. Do you get melancholy thoughts more often at particular times of day or in particular situations? Being able to identify trends will enable you to handle them proactively.

6. Honoring Minor Victories: Utilize your journal to record minor triumphs during the difficulties. Today, did you get out of bed? Did you do any task, regardless of how small? Celebrate and acknowledge these accomplishments, creating a narrative that is good.

7. Have a Compassionate Conversation

with Your Inner Self: Talk to your inner self with compassion. Compose letters to yourself with words of support, understanding, and encouragement. Think of your notebook as a confidant who offers judgment-free listening.

8. Healing Vision: Create a picture of your path

to recovery. Give a detailed description of the kind of person you want to be. Write down in your journal your ideal future scenario—one in which the burden of melancholy thoughts is progressively lifted.

9. Creative Expression: Accept that journaling

is a creative process. Make notes, sketches, or use color in your submissions. Emotions that words alone would find difficult to describe might be accessed through creative expression.

10. Expressing Gratitude in the Darkness:

Include a gratitude exercise in your notebook. Find

little things for which to be thankful, even when you're feeling down. This exercise progressively turns your attention from the gloom of your life to its glimmering light.

Concluding Remarks: When traveling through depressive thoughts, journaling is your personal travel partner. It serves as both a canvas on which you can paint the colors of your emotions and a mirror reflecting your inner world. Accept the process, practice self-compassion, and allow your notebook serve as a record of your growth and resiliency.

3b..Mindfulness Meditation

The practice of mindfulness meditation fosters acceptance of one's thoughts and feelings without passing judgment on them, as well as present-moment awareness. Let's examine the fundamentals of mindfulness meditation and how it may be an effective tool for overcoming life's obstacles.

Accepting Mindfulness in Meditation

1. The Presence Technique:

Being completely present in the here and now is the fundamental component of mindfulness meditation. It asks you to step back from your thoughts and feelings and simply observe them.

2. Setting the Scene: Look for a calm, cozy area.

Establish a space where you can concentrate inwardly without being distracted, whether it's a chair, cushion, or even just the floor.

3. Grounding in Breath: Pay attention to your

breathing at first. Observe the breathing in and out. When your thoughts stray, allow your breath to act as a stabilizing anchor, bringing you back to the here and now.

4. Non-Judgmental Observation: Keep an

open mind and notice ideas as they come to you. See the passing clouds in your mind's sky as your ideas. Although you acknowledge them, gently return your attention to the breath.

5. Body Scan: Bring your attention to your entire

body. Examine your body, focusing on every area.

This method eases tension and encourages a close relationship with your physical body.

6. Acceptance of Emotions: Whether they are happy or sad, mindfulness promotes acceptance of emotions. Feelings come up, but instead of fighting them or holding onto them, notice them and let them pass.

7. Cultivating thankfulness: Make practicing thankfulness a habit. Consider the things in your life for which you are thankful during or after your meditation. This gives your mindfulness practice a new and beneficial dimension.

8. Walking Meditation: By practicing walking meditation, you can bring mindfulness to your motions. Take pleasure in every stride and embrace the cadence of your stroll. It's a chance to incorporate mindfulness into routine tasks.

9. Mindful Eating: Change the way you think about food by engaging in mindful eating. Savor every taste of the event by using all of your senses.

This exercise cultivates a closer relationship between your body and food.

10. Adaptation to Everyday Life: Rust

Copy the programming

Expand your awareness outside of scheduled meditation sessions. Pay attention to everyday tasks like doing the dishes, driving, and standing in line. Every instant turns into a chance to practice mindfulness.

11. Show Self-Compassion: Rust

Copy the programming

Approach mindfulness with compassion for yourself. Recognize that it's acceptable for your thoughts to stray. Return to the present moment without passing judgment on yourself, and treat yourself with kindness.

12. Resources and Apps for Mindfulness:

Copy the programming

Examine sites and applications for mindfulness that provide guided meditations. These resources, which offer scheduled sessions and a variety of meditation subjects, might be helpful, especially for newcomers.

Final Thoughts:

Being mindful when you meditate is a path toward transformation, not a quick fix. It's a discipline that develops over time, progressively changing the way you relate to ideas, feelings, and the environment. Open yourself up to every moment and use mindfulness as a compass to find inner peace and resiliency.

3c: Social Connection

A vital component of human well-being, social interaction is essential for maintaining our mental and emotional stability. Let's examine the value of social interaction and the ways in which cultivating connections can be an effective strategy for overcoming obstacles in life.

The Core of Social Interaction

1. Human Need at Birth:

Our urge for social interaction is basic and encoded into our biology. Our capacity to create connections and attachments has been essential to our existence and well-being from the first human tribes to contemporary communities.

2. Emotional Support: Meaningful connections provide an emotional safety net. Having a thinking partner offers consolation and perspective when dealing with obstacles or challenging emotions.

3. Lessening Isolation: Social interaction helps to lessen isolation. It gives us a sense of community and our common humanity by serving as a reminder that we are not alone in our experiences.

4. Developing Resilience: Resilience is influenced by meaningful social ties. The encouragement and support of friends and family can help you overcome hardship and give you strength when things get hard.

5. Diverse Views: You are exposed to a variety of viewpoints and concepts when you interact with a diverse set of people. This deepens your awareness of the world, expanding your perspectives and fostering personal development.

6. Celebrating Success: Joy is increased when others share in one's accomplishments. Honoring successes, no matter how minor, in a community of friends and family strengthens a positive narrative and a feeling of achievement.

7. Handling Difficulties: Social networks can be a source of solace when things are hard. The presence of people helps lesen the weight of challenges, whether through sympathetic chats or cooperative activities.

8. Empathy and Understanding: These two qualities are the foundation of meaningful partnerships. Having other people see and hear you provides a feeling of acceptance and affirmation that enhances emotional health.

9. Benefits to Physical Health: Social interaction has a favorable effect on physical health in addition to mental health. Strong social bonds have been linked in studies to reduced stress and enhanced general wellbeing.

10. Value Superior to Volume:

The quality of the relationships matters more than their quantity. Embrace a small number of profound and significant relationships instead of chasing a large number of fleeting ones. Real assistance is given by relationships of high quality.

11. Being Present and Actively Listening:

Engage in interactions by listening intently. Deepening the connection, being really present when someone is giving their views shows that you appreciate and care about their experiences.

12. Mutually Beneficial Connections:

Positive social relationships require reciprocity. Aim for partnerships in which each side gains something from the relationship. Mutual assistance and shared experiences are strengthened through reciprocity.

13. Juggling Online and Offline Relationships:

Prioritize in-person encounters wherever you can, even though digital connections have their role. Digital communication might not fully convey the depth and richness that face-to-face encounters offer.

Final Thoughts:

Our lives are woven together by the dynamic energy of social interaction, which has a tremendous impact on our wellbeing. Developing and maintaining meaningful connections is essential to making our journey richer, more alive, and profoundly gratifying. It is not merely a tool for overcoming obstacles in life.

3d:Exercise Routine

The Exercise Routine becomes a powerful ally, a means of regaining the joy of movement, and a gradual path toward mental well-being when it comes to combating depressive thoughts.

Setting Out on a Movement Adventure:
Your workout regimen is an exploration of movement as medicine, not just a series of physical tasks. Imagine it as a journey where every step is a

purposeful move toward getting back your vitality and control.

Exercise can be thought of as a dance of liberation. Every yoga stance, every run, and every stretch offers a chance for release—a letting go of any burden that depressive thoughts could hold. It's a dance that releases the bonds of negativity from the body and the mind.

Finding the Gentle Flow: Your exercise regimen doesn't have to be a strenuous physical exercise; it can just be a flow of movements that make you feel good about yourself. Let the simple act of stretching or the contemplative stroll in the outdoors provide a reassuring rhythm that corresponds with your emotional requirements.

Taking Care of Your Inner plant: Just as a plant needs gentle attention to grow, exercising gives your emotional health the loving care it needs to thrive. Every session turns into an act of self-love and a dedication to creating a durable and colorful mental landscape.

Chasing Away the Shadows: Moving your body is a conscious effort to chase away shadows rather than just a physical activity. Imagine the pumping of your heart and the contraction of your muscles as a symbolic clearing of the clouds over your mind.

Partnership in Motion: Think about making physical activity a travel companion. Join a group or extend an invitation to a friend. A layer of support is added by the shared experience, transforming individual steps into a group investigation of well-being. Talks while on a brisk stroll or giggles during a fitness class wave together to form a web of connection.

After the physical exertion, give yourself some time for focused rest and reflection. It's not just about collecting your breath; it's also about taking a moment to consider the strength you've mustered and to celebrate your victories, no matter how minor. Allow the echoes of success to fill your thoughts.

A Symphony of Self-Care: Working out is a symphony of self-care, not a chore. Every step you take, every conscious decision you make to exercise, adds to the composition of a tune that speaks to your emotional health.

Recall that an exercise regimen is a powerful tool in your toolbox to combat melancholy thoughts rather than a panacea. Discover a hint of resiliency in each step and a whisper of self-love with each stretch. Allow this routine to transform into a dance, an adventure, and a celebration of your inner power.

3e:Goal-setting

Setting Sail with Purpose
Moving through the terrain of conquering melancholy thoughts requires purposeful direction in addition to mobility. Together, we will examine how to use goal-setting as a mental compass to steer you toward greater possibilities.

The Clarity Power: Creating objectives is akin to honing the lens through which you see your future. When your goals are clear, it's easier to express what you hope to accomplish and to create a clear path through the mist of doubt.

Getting Past the Inertia Trap: Objectives serve as impetus for action. The bonds of inactivity that melancholy thoughts could impose are broken by them. By stating your goals clearly, you give your trip direction and give yourself more impetus.

Small Wins, Big Impact: Think about dividing more ambitious objectives into more doable, smaller ones. In addition to making the road easier to handle, these bite-sized goals also offer a series of minor victories that add up to a feeling of advancement and success.

Increasing Motivation: Objectives serve as sources of inspiration. They are the beacons that help you get through times of uncertainty or exhaustion. Setting goals can ignite a fire within you and give you newfound vigor to pursue your objectives.

Flexibility in Aspiration: While establishing clear objectives is essential, be flexible in pursuing them. Because life is a dynamic adventure, things can change. Give yourself liberty to modify your objectives so that they continue to be reasonable and in line with your changing demands.

Objectives can be both physical and intangible. Aspirations can be both. Realistic objectives could be things like finishing a project or picking up a new skill. Intangible objectives, like practicing gratitude or developing self-compassion, explore the emotional domain and enhance your inner landscape.

Mental Vision Board: Arrange your objectives into a mental vision board. Visualize your desired state of affairs, your desired emotions, and the achievements you hope to attain. This visualization turns into a strong motivator that draws you in the direction of the picture you've drawn for yourself.

Recognizing Milestones: Take time to acknowledge your progress as you work toward your objectives. Acknowledge your improvement and enjoy your sense of accomplishment. This is more than simply a pat on the back—it's an acknowledgement of your perseverance and dedication.

Accountability and Support: Discuss your objectives with a therapist, family member, or close friend. Having a responsible party at your side might be motivating when things go tough. Their help acts as an anchor to keep you steady while you pursue your goals.

Thought and Modifications: Consider your objectives on a regular basis. Evaluate what is effective and what may require modification. Reflection is a continuous process of learning and improving your path toward well-being rather than a means of passing judgment.

Goals become more than just destinations on the path to conquering depressed thoughts—they become guiding beacons. Every objective you set for yourself turns into a pledge to a better tomorrow and a monument to your power.

3f: Cognitive Behavioral Techniques

Thinking Clearly and Compassionately:
Cognitive Behavioral Strategies
Cognitive Behavioral Techniques (CBT) become a kind mentor when it comes to combating depressive

thoughts, assisting you in comprehending and reshaping the complex mental terrain.

Studying the Thought Terrain: Cognitive Behavioral Therapy (CBT) encourages you to investigate your mental landscape. Understanding, not judgment, is the key. Think of CBT as a kind compass that guides you curiously around the huge landscape that is your mind.

Recognizing Thought Trends:

Start by figuring out mental processes. The goal of CBT is to help you identify recurrent themes in your thoughts. Exist any recurring negative self-talk patterns or presumptions about the future? The basis for transformation is this self-awareness.

CBT is your buddy when it comes to dispelling unfavorable presumptions. When an idea comes to mind, consider its viability. Exist contrasting viewpoints? It promotes a more balanced perspective and is akin to being a detective looking at the evidence proving or disproving a certain idea.

Using Mindfulness in Thought Observation:
Bring awareness into your observations of thoughts.

Keep your mind clear of your ideas and view them from a distance. Think of your ideas as passing clouds; you are the sky, unchanged, noticing the fleeting patterns.

Rewriting and Reframing Narratives:
Cognitive Behavioral Therapy promotes the skill of reframing. When negative ideas start to creep in, try rephrasing them into more realistic or upbeat stories. Instead of downplaying your emotions, try rewriting the narratives you tell yourself to create a more compassionate inner monologue.

Building a Thought Toolbox: Create a thought toolbox. Stuff it full of inspirational sayings, affirmations, and happy pictures. When confronted with difficult ideas, use your toolkit for affirmations that promote optimism and fortitude. It's your own particular defense system against pessimism.

Accepting Self-Compassion: CBT provides a means of fostering self-compassion. Navigate your ideas with kindness. Think of yourself as you would a buddy going through a similar situation. Self-compassion turns into the salve that heals the injuries caused by pessimistic thinking.

Progress, Not Perfection: CBT emphasizes progress over perfection. Appreciate the little triumphs, the times you refute a false belief or write a story. Every stride demonstrates your increasing command of your mental terrain.

Using Expert Advice as a Compass: Take into account obtaining expert advice. A CBT-trained therapist can serve as your reliable guide, offering strategies and insights specific to your personal path. Their assistance turns into a guiding light as you negotiate the complexities of your thoughts.

Using the Techniques in Daily Life: Easily integrate CBT into your day-to-day activities. Include strategies in times of reflection or when confronted with difficult circumstances. When CBT is applied consistently, it costs to be a tool and becomes a natural part of your mental navigation.

Cognitive Behavioral Techniques are strands of comprehension and change in the fabric of conquering depressed ideas. They give you the ability to actively participate in changing the stories that are being told inside, creating a mental environment that is kinder and more resilient than before.

3g:Art and Creativity

Painting Resilience with Colors: Creativity and Art
Art and creativity appear as bright colors on the canvas of conquering depression-inducing thoughts, giving you the ability to freely express yourself and use healing techniques to paint your path with deep emotional insights.

The Canvas of Self-Expression: When words fail, art steps in to fill the void. Painting, drawing, or sculpture are examples of non-verbal communication that can be used to convey the complex feelings that are present. Every stroke turns into an internal conversation in silence.

Creativity encourages you to go beyond the bounds of language in your exploration. Explore the realm of shapes, colors, and images. It's an investigation that lets the true nature of your feelings come to the surface without requiring exact words.

Catharsis in the Arts: Producing art is a therapeutic process. It's about the creative process itself, not about the finished masterpiece. You let go of emotions when you create art; you bring them to the surface and give them room to air.

Pain to Beauty: Pain can be alchemically transformed into beauty through the creative process. The intense feelings are transformed into visually arresting art, whether it's via the energetic dance of a dancer or the vibrant brushstrokes of a painter.

Accepting Imperfections: Being creative is a celebration of flaws. It's more important to embrace your expression's individuality than to live up to society's expectations of perfection. What some may consider imperfections in art become the distinguishing features of uniqueness.

Art as a Mirror:
The depths of your emotions are reflected in the mirrors you create. Looking at your work presents you with a picture of what's going on within. It's a

mirror that encourages understanding and introspection.

Playful Exploration: Take a playful, exploratory approach to art. Let go of expectations, regardless of your experience level as an artist. Let your imagination run wild without inhibitions. This playfulness is where surprising beauty frequently appears.

Using Art to Start Conversations: If you feel comfortable doing so, show off your artwork to people. Art transcends spoken communication and becomes a topic of conversation. It creates an opening for understanding and connection by allowing people into your inner world.

Lead by Intuition: Permit your creative process to be led by intuition. Trust your instincts when selecting hus, forms, or motions. Intuition be comes the compass on a creative trip that takes you through unfamiliar emotional terrain.

Including Art in Daily Routines: Include art in your everyday routines. Let creativity become a constant companion on your path to emotional well-being, whether it takes a few minutes to sketch, a dance in your living room, or working with clay.

Art and creativity play a vital role in the symphony of conquering depression thoughts. They provide a means of expression as well as a transformational force that encourages self-discovery, healing, and the freedom to paint your emotional landscape in the cues of resilience.

3h:Gratitude Practice

Creating Radiance Gratitude Practice is a beautiful flower that blooms in the garden of emotional well-being, inviting you to cultivate appreciation, mindfulness, and a subtle shift in perspective.

The process of cultivating gratitude is akin to sowing the seeds of mindfulness. It's about appreciating beauty in the little things and living in the present. Every thankful moment is a seed that, with care, blossoms into a positive garden.

Harvests of Gratitude Every Day: Every day, cultivate gratitude. Take a moment every day to consider your blessings. It may be a tiny gesture, a belly laugh, or the sun's warmth. You can develop the habit of finding the good even when faced with difficulties by regularly praising these instances.

Changing Your Attention from Lack to Abundance: Gratitude is a kind prod to help you change your attention from what you lack to the abundance that is all around you. It's a reminder that there are things in life to be grateful for, even during trying times. This small but meaningful realization leads to a transformation in viewpoint.

Create a Gratitude Journal: You might want to think about starting one. Set aside some time every day to write down your blessings. This habit serves as a concrete reminder of the abundance in your life and not only captures special moments; it also acts as a lighthouse in the darkest circumstances.

Giving Thanks to Others: Being grateful goes beyond only thinking about oneself. Tell people how much you appreciate them. Express sincere gratitude to loved ones, friends, and complete strangers who have impacted your life. Positive energy spreads via this reciprocal act of giving and receiving gratitude.

Savoring Moments of delight: Expreciating moments of delight and being grateful go hand in hand. Give yourself time to thoroughly enjoy moments when you come upon something lovely or touching. Allow the happiness to stay with you and leave a lasting impression that will make you grateful.

Gratitude is the art of looking for positive aspects in difficult circumstances. It doesn't minimize problems; instead, it encourages you to look for the good or lessons in them. You can overcome misfortune with gratitude and resilience when you use this thoughtful approach.

Gratitude Rituals in Everyday Life: Make gratitude rituals a part of your everyday existence. These practices, which include giving thanks before meals, recognizing the sunrise, and taking time to enjoy the outdoors, establish gratitude as an essential component of your daily life.

Thinking Back on Personal Development: Being grateful encompasses personal development. Think back on your path and be thankful for the knowledge you've received, the resilience you've shown, and the person you've become. Gratitude and self-compassion become more deeply connected as a result of this reflection.

Being grateful goes beyond practice and becomes a way of life. Instill a grateful mindset in your life, where admiration for the intricate details and beauty of your life arises naturally.

Gratitude Practice becomes a graceful companion in the dance of conquering depression thoughts, helping you to recognize the light both inside and around you, cultivating a garden of resilience and a heart full of gratitude.

3i: Routine and Structure

Using Structure and Routine to Anchor Stability
Routine and structure stand out as strong pillars in the emotional well-being fabric, offering consistency, predictability, and a solid base on which to develop resilience.

Establishing Daily Rhythms: Your routine is the song that guides your day. Create daily routines by designating specific hours for eating, sleeping, working, and relaxing. This steady pulse becomes a reassuring heartbeat that keeps you rooted through life's ups and downs.

A Sanctuary of Predictability: A sanctuary of predictability is established by structure. Maintaining a controlled environment helps one feel in control in an uncertain world. It's the structure that gives you a greater feeling of direction as you go through each day.

Managing Responsibilities and Rest: Establish a routine that is both responsible and restorative. Make time for your studies or employment, recreational pursuits, and getting enough sleep. This balance protects your wellbeing and guarantees that you fulfill your responsibilities.

Concise Transitions: Construct conscious shifts from one activity to another. These breaks serve as bridges, enabling you to move from one work to another with awareness and purpose, whether it's a quick walk or a moment of deep breathing.

Flexibility within Structure: Although structure is essential, give it some leeway. Because life is dynamic, unforeseen things can happen. Give yourself permission to modify your regimen as necessary so long as it stays a helpful structure rather than a strict requirement.

Developing Personal Rituals: Include personal rituals in your daily activities. These rituals become anchors, offering a sense of security and continuity, whether they are morning routines that establish a positive tone for the day or evening routines that indicate a shift to relaxation.

Making Self-Care a Priority: Include self-care in your everyday routine. Make time for the things that make you happy and reenergized. It could be just some peaceful time for reading, contemplation, meditation, or a hobby. Making self-care a priority strengthens your emotional fortitude.

Making Use of Time Blocks: Take into account setting aside time for different tasks. Organizing your day into focused blocks will increase productivity and help you avoid feeling overwhelmed. It releases you from the burden of a full day's worth of obligations, allowing you to focus on particular tasks.

Setting Objectives in a Routine:

Include goal-setting in your daily routine. Having a defined direction within the framework of your routine gives you a sense of purpose and success, whether your goals are daily, weekly, or monthly.

Morning and Evening Reflections: Make time each day for reflections in the morning and the evening. Begin each day with an expression of appreciation and intention, and end it with a quick recap of your successes and happy moments. With awareness, frame your day with these contemplative exercises.

Routine and structure come together to form a harmonious dance in the choreography of conquering melancholy thoughts, offering a sense of stability and order. They act as a blank canvas that you may fill with the hues of your everyday existence, creating a rhythm that supports both emotional health and productivity.

3j:Professional Support

Leading Light: Expert Assistance
Professional support is a guiding light in the emotional well-being mosaic, providing knowledge, compassion, and a cooperative path to recovery.

Recognizing Your Strength to Ask for Help:
Asking for help from a professional is a sign of strength, not weakness. It's a recognition that you should receive committed coaching and knowledge as you go toward emotional health.

Therapy as a Safe Haven: Therapy turns into a place where you can feel understood and empathetically shared about your thoughts, feelings, and experiences. A therapist offers a private setting where you can examine, communicate, and sort out the complexity inside of you.

Collaborative Exploration: Receiving professional support entails working together to explore your feelings and difficulties. You set out on a journey with a therapist to comprehend patterns, recognize coping mechanisms, and create a toolkit for enduring life's ups and downs.

Customized Methods for Specific Requirements: Experts provide customized methods to address your particular requirements. The advice is tailored to fit your unique journey, whether it is cognitive-behavioral therapy, psychoanalysis, or another therapeutic modality.

When Appropriate, Medication Management: Physicians may occasionally advise medication as a component of a treatment plan. When necessary, medication management is carried out under close supervision to ensure that it enhances other therapeutic approaches and maximizes your well-being.

Validation and Empowerment: Both are given by professional assistance. The road involves more than just overcoming obstacles; it also involves developing resilience, realizing your abilities, and gaining the courage to handle life's obstacles head-on.

Crisis Intervention and Support: Expert assistance acts as a crucial stabilizing force in times of crisis. Therapists are qualified to intervene right away, giving you a safety net to help you through difficult times.

Developing Coping Strategies: Experts assist you in developing coping mechanisms. Whether it's cultivating stress management techniques, effective communication skills, or mindfulness practices, these strategies become tools for everyday life.

Frequent Check-Ins and Progress Assessments: Part of providing professional help is conducting frequent check-ins and progress assessments. It is a dynamic procedure in which your changing requirements and milestones are used to continuously refine the therapeutic journey.

Promoting Ongoing Growth: The objective of expert assistance goes beyond handling emergencies; it promotes ongoing development. Therapists collaborate with you to establish objectives, promote self-awareness, and develop a plan for sustained emotional health.

In the embrace of professional support, you find a friend who walks along you, offering support, empowerment, and a steady hand as you make your way towards resilience and healing. This friend also understands the nuances of your emotional landscape.

Chapter 4: Tools for Anxiety

Anxiety frequently takes center stage in the complex dance of emotional well-being, obscuring the present. This chapter provides an overview of Tools for Anxiety, which offers strategies for resolving difficult and unsettling situations.

4a. Deep Breathing Techniques:

Deep breathing techniques are a calming melody that may be heard in the emotional well-being symphony, providing a haven for those experiencing stress and worry. Let's investigate these practices as a kind of roadmap for traversing inner serenity.

**1. Box Breathing: Inducing Breath Symmetry

Breathe in for four counts, hold it for four counts, release it for four counts, and then wait for an additional four counts.

Imagine using your breath to trace the sides of a box. Your breathing will become symmetrical as a result of this regular pattern, which also balances and calms the nervous system.

**2. The Breath of Serenity: Diaphragmatic Breathing

Grasp your abdomen with one hand and your chest with the other. Breathe deeply through your nose, letting your stomach grow. With your lips pursed, gently release the breath as you feel your belly constrict.

By using the diaphragm, this exercise encourages keeper breathing, which tells the body to relax. It grounds you in the here and now and is like a breath of fresh air.

3. 4-7-8 Breathing: The Peaceful Lullaby

Breathe in gently via your nose for four counts, hold it for seven counts, and then release the breathe loudly through your mouth for eight counts.

This method serves as a lullaby for the nervous system and was made popular by Dr. Andrew Weil. The long exhale has a calming effect that invites peace of mind and body.

4. Changing Up Your Nostril Breathing: Balancing Energy

Using your thumb to close your right nostril, take a breath through your left. With your ring finger closed, open your right nostril, and let out a breath. Breathe in through your right nostril, shut it, let go of your left, and then exhale.

By balancing the body's energy flow, this yoga pose helps people feel clear and balanced. It's a harmonious breath that unites the two internal energy.

**5. Harmonizing Your Breath with Your Heartbeat

Establish a breathing rhythm that feels comfortable, ideally six breaths per minute. Five counts of inhalation and five counts of exhalation.

Your heartbeat and resonant breathing work together to produce a rhythmic pattern. This practice brings your heart and breath into alignment, which promotes peace and harmony.

**6. Mindful Breathing: Consciousness with Every Breath

Just focus on taking deep, steady breaths. Take note of how each breath in and out feels. Pay attention to the movement of air in your nostrils or the rise and fall of your chest.

Breathing mindfully is an exercise in awareness alone. The mind gradually untangles from distractions as you concentrate on each breath, promoting a calm and focused state.

These deep breathing exercises are calls to develop a relationship with your breath, a powerful ally in navigating the calm inside the anxiety-inducing storm. They are more than just tactics. You etch a path to resilience and calmness with every deliberate breath.

4b.Progressive Muscle Relaxation

Progressive Muscle Relaxation: Releasing Stress, Promoting Serenity
Progressive Muscle Relaxation (PMR) is a delicate yet powerful thread that weaves itself through the emotional well-being fabric, assisting you in releasing tension and developing a deep sense of peace. Together, let's investigate this method as a careful examination of the terrain of your body.

**1. Locating Your Comfort Zone

Firstly, locate a peaceful and cozy area. Allow your body to find a comfortable and supportive sitting or lying position. If closing your eyes helps you feel more at ease, then do so.

**2. Become Aware of Your Breath

Give your breathing some attention for a short while. Breathe in deeply through your nose, letting your belly rise, and then softly release the breath through your mouth. Let a feeling of peace surround you with every breath.

**3. Raising Conscience from the Toe to the Head

Point your focus on your toes first. Tense your toe muscles gently as you inhale, and retain the tension for a short while. Next, remove all of the tension by exhaling. Observe the difference between stress and ease.

**4. Directing the Relaxation Wave Upward

Gradually raise your awareness throughout your body, focusing on various muscle groups each time. The soft wave of tension is applied to the calves, thighs, belly, chest, shoulders, arms, neck, and face, and then it is released.

**5. Accepting the Release Harmony

Observe the sensations of tension and release that occur after activating each muscle group. With every inhalation, release any remaining tension and allow your body to give into a deep state of relaxation.

**6.Progressive Muscle Relaxations

Progressive Muscle Relaxation is a mindful presence technique in addition to physical release. Feel every muscle group in your body as you move through it, paying close attention to the minute changes in feeling and the ensuing calm.

**7. Harmony Across the Body

To finish the journey, tense your entire body for a short moment, releasing the tension entirely after creating a gentle wave from your toes to your head.

Feel the harmony of calm coursing through your whole being.

**8.Relishing in the Afterglow

Spend a few moments basking in the relaxation's aftereffects. Let your body bask in the peace that Progressive Muscle Relaxation has brought about, allowing it to absorb it all.

You proceed on a thoughtful journey with Progressive Muscle Relaxation's cadence, urging your body to release tension and accept inner peace. With every deliberate to release, you create a peaceful oasis where the effects of tension fade away, leaving a canvas covered with peace.

4c:Grounding Techniques

Grounding Methods: Staying Fixed in the Here and Now
Grounding strategies are like rock solid anchors in the tides of emotional health, providing a lifeline

through stressful and anxious times. Let's examine these methods as a kind of gentle instruction on how to ground yourself in the here and now.

**1. 4-3-3-2-1 Method: Using Your Senses

List the following: five visual senses, four tactile senses, three auditory senses, two olfactory senses, and one taste sense.

By using your senses, this approach helps you bring your awareness into the present. It serves as a link between you and the material elements of your environment, giving you a sense of anchoring.

**2. Breath Counting: Aligning Breath with Numerical Expressions

Breathe in gently for four counts, hold it for four counts, release it for four counts, and then wait for an additional four counts.

By combining breathing with counting, you can stay anchored in the here and now. A constant cadence is created by the intentional attention on breathing and numbers, which helps to concentrate your awareness and relax your mind.

**3. Body Scan: Examining Sensations of the Body

Mentally scan your body, paying attention to each area, beginning at your toes. With each breath, picture releasing any tension or discomfort you may have noticed. By establishing a link between your body and mind, this approach helps you stay rooted in the current moment's physical experiences.

**4. Nature Connection: Taking in the Outside Environment

Go outside or peer through a window. Take note of the surrounding environment, including the sky, clouds, and trees. Take note of the hues, patterns, and motions. This relationship with nature grounds you in the splendor of the outside world and offers a tranquil backdrop.

**5. Sensorial Touchstones: Grounding Objects

Carry a little, textured item with you, such as a smooth pebble, a stone, or a piece of cloth. Feel the object's weight and texture with your hands while you're feeling nervous. This concrete bond acts as a reassuring anchor, offering solace and steadiness.

**6. Walking With Awareness: A Mindful Approach

If you can, take a quick stroll. Feel the connection between your feet and the ground with every step. Take note of your walking gait, the feel of your muscles, and the minute changes in your weight. By purposeful movement, mindful walking helps you focus your attention in the here and now.

**7. Positive Statements with a Positive Foundation

Make a list of encouraging and validating remarks. Remind yourself of these statements whenever you're feeling nervous. This exercise grounds you in a resilient attitude, counteracts nervous thoughts, and strengthens positivity.

**8. Image Anchors: Establishing Safe Havens for the Mind

Imagine yourself in a peaceful, secure environment, such as a cozy room, a beach, or a forest. Shut your eyes and let the subtleties of this mental haven absorb you. Imagery anchors let you ground yourself in the calming environment of your mind and bring you to a place of calmness.

You find a palette of tools inside the tapestry of grounding techniques that allow you to anchor in the here and now. Every method is a brushstroke that creates a calm canvas inside of which the stress and anxiety currents slowly recede.

4d:Positive Affirmations

 Alleviation Source Maintaining the Positive Aspects of Your Nursery In the main success theater , positive declarations cub like robust flowers, each petal prepared to promote the structure of solid foundations for an active internal strategy. The purpose of this session is to encourage the development of a confident inner nursery through the use of positive documentations.

" I am Extreme"

Take a hard look at your internal inflexibility. This ad age should always be flashed back when circumstances feel questionable and you need to have confidence in your capability to go through them.

" I Embrace Change and Advancement"

Consider life as an ongoing trial. Recite this as a pivotal part of an occasion to help you embrace the perspective that views change as an occasion for mindfulness.

" I really rate Love and protestation"

suppose on your natural worth. lose sight of the ways that you earn support, love, and empathy from both other people and from yourself.

" I Choose Happiness and Joy"

cover your right to happiness. Remind yourself to keep an auspicious station on life and to designedly seek fulfillment.

" I am Equipped and Sure"

Make use of this protestation to strengthen your conviction. Recall your advantages and develop a stronger sense of tone- assurance in your capacities.

" I Attract Sure Energy and entries"

Make that decision grounded on what you wish to attract into your life. Say this mantra to yourself to let positive energy and possibilities enter into your life.

" I Conveyance Negative Contemplations and Embrace Energy"

To let go of judgment, use this protestation. Consider it a memorial to let go of your tone-preservation and mistrustfulness in order to make room for energy.

" I am Grateful for Each Day"

Use this attesting document to cultivate appreciation. Give gratefulness for everything in your life, especially this present right now.

" I Trust the Journey of Life"

Trust the path your life ison.However, we should accept that you might be suitable to overcome problems while still having a clear anticipation, If anything is unclear.

" I am a Reference point of Light and Energy"

Emphasize how you're a major influence. fantasize yourself as a light source that illuminates the area girding you.

Ways to Get Stirred Up to Work
Choose declarations that really reverberate with you. Say many times a day, either out loud or discreetly. bandy each assertion with confidence and assurance. Sort them out in the canny twinkles and assessments. declarations can be modified and acclimatized to your changing requirements. Think of your wants as seeds that sow into a chastened, concentrated, and gratified theater . With each emphasis, you produce a specific internal scene for yourself.

4e: Visualization: Show Off Your Path to Joy

On the canvas of emotional well-being, visualization functions as a paintbrush, inviting you to boldly create your idealized reality. We'll look at visualization techniques together to help you create a confident, upbeat, and happy mental image of your ideal self.

**1. Setting the Scene: Choosing a Quiet Place

First, choose a quiet, comfortable place. Either lie down or sit in a comfortable position. To avoid outside distractions, close your eyes and allow your mind to travel inside.

**2. Take Deep Breaths: Exhale Calm, Release Tension

Take a few deep breaths to help you focus yourself. Breathe in slowly through your nose, allowing your belly to expand, and then gently exhale through your mouth to release any remaining tension. With every breath, you become grounded in the present moment.

**3. Choosing Your Own Picture: A Particular Case

Select a situation that you would like to find yourself in: reaching a personal best, getting through a challenging situation, or accomplishing a goal.

Make everything positive, hopeful, and in line with your objectives.

4. Creating Detailed Illustrations by Using the Senses

As you visualize your scene, make use of all your senses. What is it that you can see, hear, feel, smell, and maybe even taste in this realm of your mind? To create a multisensory experience, strive for the highest level of vivacity and detail in the visuals.

5. Bringing Joy and Self-Belief: Bringing Positive Feelings

Connect with the joyous emotions your visualization evoked. Allow your thoughts to be filled with the emotions you are feeling, such as success, happiness, or confidence. Feel them as though they are happening right now.

6. Assuming the Mantle of the Hero: Achieving Your Dream

See yourself as the confident, capable lead character in your own narrative, possessing all the qualities you have always wanted. Visualize yourself winning, overcoming challenges, and shining with joy.

**7. Event Order: Observing Success

Visualize the series of actions in your chosen scenario that will result in achievement. With assurance and clarity, picture each step in your mind. Imagine yourself facing challenges head-on with courage and celebrating your progress along the way.

**8. Using Affirmations in Visualization to Strengthen Positively

Incorporate words of encouragement into your images. Repeat affirmations that are relevant to your circumstances to bolster your confidence and self-belief.

**9. Concluding Remarks and Thank Yous: Reviewing the Experience

As your visualization comes to a conclusion, express gratitude for the delightful experience. Reflect on the emotions and insights you experienced during the visualization, noting that positive outcomes can be influenced by your ideas.

**10. Integrating into Daily Activities: Consistency Is Key

Regularly use imagery into your everyday tasks. Use it frequently, particularly when you're feeling down or are setting objectives or introspecting. The more visualization exercises you do, the more effective it becomes as a tool for changing your reality and way of thinking.

By learning the art of visualization, you can build a successful, resilient, and happy mental landscape. You use your creativity to create your path to optimism, creating a vision that aligns with your highest goals and brings you one step closer to your ideal reality.

4f: Time Management

How to Manage Your Time to Be further Productive In the diurnal distraction of life, time operation becomes a compass that guides you through the highs and lows of liabilities, precedences, and particular good. We will look at time operation ways to see how to strike a balance between the demands of productivity and your overall health.

** 1. Determining Clear Precedences

Bringing Your Focus Up Prioritize your top precedences first. easily define your pretensions, both immediate and long- term. Focus on the tasks that align with these precedences to ensure that your diurnal conditioning are helping you achieve your overall pretensions.

** 2. Creating an Conditioning List Making a

Chart of the Journey Make a list of tasks for everyday or every week. To make a diurnal schedule, divide your tasks into manageable gobbets. This palpable list acts as a roadmap to help you stay systematized and motivated.

** 3. Prioritization The Art of Task Ordering

Arrange the jobs grounded on their urgency and precedence. Make use of fabrics like the Eisenhower Matrix, which classify jobs into four groups: not critical nor critical, not critical nor critical, critical and important, and critical and critical. You can more manage the time you spend on tasks by using this strategy.

** 4. Time Management Putting Your Day in Order

You should record distinct times throughout the day for certain tasks or orders. By allocating particular time for tasks, you can increase productivity and drop distractions by employing a system known as time blocking.

** 5. The Pomodoro Method fastening Bursts

Use the Pomodoro fashion, which assigns you to work hard for a set period of time(generally 25 twinkles) and also take a brief break. These focused sprints help you produce an authority that maximizes your time and energy while aiding you in maintaining focus and precluding weariness.

** 6. Develop Your Delegation Capabilities

Shared Accounts   Identify the jobs that can be assigned. Delegation not only gives people more power but also frees up your time to concentrate on effects that fit your precedences and areas of capability. Delegating is a pivotal element of effective time operation.

**** 7. Breaks Revitalizing Your Energy** Put deliberate pauses in your timetable. These little breaks which may be a perambulation, some deep breathing exercises, or some alone time for reflection — restore your energy and enhance your overall good, precluding collapse.

**** 8. Digital Purification freeing for Clarity** Set away specified hours to indulge in your digital detox. By setting out specific ages to only use social media, emails, and announcements, you may produce continued work blocks that ameliorate internal clarity.

**** 9. Reflect and estimate non stop enhancement**
Regularly assess your time operation strategies. Examine what worked and identify what needs to be bettered. By doing this introspective exercise, you might upgrade your plan and acclimatize to shifting demands and challenges.

**** 10. Accomplishments with honor** Promoting a positive outlook Honor and express gratefulness for all of your achievements, no matter how big or small. Borrow a positive mindset by celebrating your successes. This happiness serves as provocation and a source of accomplishment.

 Consider your road to time operation as a cotillion , a metrical interplay of duties, precedences, and general well- being. You produce a healthy balance that honors both your particular and professional lives as you precisely plan, concentrate, and acclimate to ride the walls of product.

4g: Limiting Stimulants

Promoting Equilibrium and Welfare
Limiting stimulants creates a harmonizing note in the symphony of daily life, promoting well being and balance. Together, we will examine how to moderate stimulants in a way that will support your mental and physical well-being and enable you to face the challenges of daily life with vigor and resilience.

1. Knowledge of Stimulants: Being Aware Is Essential

Start by being aware of the stimulants that you encounter every day. Recognize chemicals that could affect your neurological system, such as tobacco, coffee, and some medications. Intentional moderation is built upon this understanding.

2. Cautiously Consuming Coffee: Drinking with Awareness

Be careful when consuming caffeinated beverages. Be aware of how much caffeine you consume and how it could affect your sleep and energy levels. If you want to prevent your sleep patterns from being disturbed, think about putting limitations on the amount and timing of coffee you consume.

3. Balanced Diet: Providing Your Body with Appropriate Fuel

Continue eating a wholesome, well-balanced diet. Make sure that the vital vitamins and minerals, healthy fats, carbs, and protein are all included in your meals. A body that is well-fed is more capable of managing stress and day-to-day difficulties without the need for stimulants.

**4. Hydration: Water's Power

Make staying hydrated a priority by consuming enough water throughout the day. Staying well hydrated promotes general health and helps you sustain your energy levels naturally without the need for stimulants.

**5. Rest as a Restorative Practice: Getting Good Sleep

Set aside time for good sleep as a vital component of overall health. Establish a regular sleep pattern, set up a nightly ritual, and improve your sleeping surroundings. Getting enough sleep lessens the need for stimulants to fight off exhaustion.

**6. Natural Energy Enhancers: Utilizing the Environment

Investigate natural strategies to increase your energy. Spend brief moments in the outdoors, let in natural light, and partake in sensory-engaging activities. The presence of these organic energies helps maintain energy levels without the use of synthetic stimulants.

7. Stress Reduction and Mindfulness: Calming the Nervous System

Include mindfulness exercises in your daily routine. Deep breathing techniques, yoga, and meditation all assist to relax the nervous system and lessen the demand for stimulants in reaction to stress.

8. Frequent Exercise: Reviving the Body

Continue your usual workout regimen. Engaging in physical activity gives the body energy, improves mood, and benefits general wellbeing. Frequent exercise can help you become less dependent on stimulants when you need a rapid energy boost.

9. Gradual Reduction: A Methodical Procedure

If your goal is to cut back on stimulants, think about reducing them gradually. Make reasonable plans and cut back on your consumption gradually over time. This prevents sudden shifts and enables your body and mind to adjust.

10. Expert Advice: Getting Help When You Need It

If cutting back on stimulants presents difficulties for you or if you have health issues, you might want to consult a doctor. Speak with a nutritionist or healthcare professional to develop a customized plan that fits your health objectives.

Imagine your journey of cutting back on stimulants as a symphony, with each piece harmonizing to produce a vivid, well-balanced composition. By making conscious decisions, eating healthily, and being self-aware, you develop a way of living that enhances your health and gives you the energy and fortitude to move through life's rhythms.

4h: Self- compassion practices

Creating a Caring Environment Self- compassion practices plant the seeds of kindness in the delicate soil of emotional well- being. Let's examine how rehearsing tone- compassion can help one develop compassion for themselves and accept both their dark and light sides.

**** 1. purposeful Self- Compassion** Meditation fastening on the Present   Start with a tone-compassionate, focused contemplation. detect a peaceful area, shut your eyes, and concentrate on your breathing. Take a deep breath, also release it with acceptance of your true tone. Remind yourself to be kind to yourself and accept that excrescencies are a natural part of being mortal with each breath.

** 2. Writing in Your Journal with Self-Compassionate Speech

As you write in your tablet, flash back to be kind to yourself. Without passing judgment, put your passions and studies on jotting. When you witness tone- review, respond to it with love and empathy. This exercise promotes soul-searching and a kind internal discussion.

** 3. Self- Compassion Breaks Acts of Kindness in the Face of Adversity

Spend some time rehearsing tone- compassion during grueling situations. Just take a moment to accept that challenges will always arise in life. Tell yourself, please, that" I am then for myself; this is tough right now." This timely response offers a sympathetic standpoint in the face of difficulties.

** 4. The tone- Clinch Method An Act of Kindness Grounded on Movement

Apply the tone- clinch system. Give yourself a soft clinch by encircling your arms around yourself. Take in the reassuring warmth of this touch. You feel secure because you're fostering kindness and tone- love by doing this small act.

** 5. Developing Self- Reach Through Loving- Kindness Contemplation to Inspire Compassion

Try fastening on compassion for both yourself and other people during a loving- kindness contemplation. Imagine yourself extending a circle of kindness to all of your musketeers, family, and indeed people you may not get along with. A further comprehensive sense of good is corroborated by this simple compassion.

** 6. Good Seeds attesting Expressions of Self- Compassion

Make a list of declarations that express tone- compassion." I embrace my defects with kindness" or' ' I'm good of love and understanding" are exemplifications of declarations that can be sown.

Say these audibly a lot to yourself to cultivate tone-compassion.

** 7. Mild Physical test experimental Chops

Take a moment to check your body smoothly and concentrate on tone- compassion. Allow compassion to percolate every area of your body as you tend to its numerous aspects. Treat any pressure or discomfort you're passing gently, feting and letting go of each feeling.

** 8. Touching with Self- Compassion Calm Movements

Touch yourself to feel better about yourself. Put your win over your heart or cover your face with a warm cloth. These comforting conduct are a physical incarnation of tone- compassion and offer comfort in trying circumstances.

** 9. Authorization Slips furnishing a Detailed Understanding for Yourself

To help you with your tone- compassion conditioning, make" authorization slips". These might be written down or they can be internal declarations that give you authorization to be mortal, make crimes, and face obstacles head- on with confidence in your identity. Adaptability and tone- remission are fostered by this approach.

** 10. Imaginary Support for imaging a Guidance Manual

Imagine a tutor who's understanding, whether they're real or not. Imagine this tutor furnishing direction and support when effects get tough. Having access to this loving energy offers still another degree of backing.

By rehearsing tone- compassion, you can produce a calm retreat inside of yourself where kindness serves as a lamp of stopgap while you navigate the highs and lows of life. Accept these ways one step at a time, feting that tone- compassion practice gradationally creates an internal shade of acceptance and warmth.

4i: Anxiety Journaling

Writing in an Anxiety Journal: Converting Fears into Knowledge

Anxiety journaling becomes a transforming tool in the context of emotional well-being; it's a sacred place where anxieties are transformed into wisdom. Let's examine the practice of anxiety journaling as a means of comprehending, navigating, and eventually overcoming anxiety with resilience.

**1. Daily Check-In on Anxiety: Respecting Your Feelings

Start by doing a daily anxiety check-in in your journal. Consider your present emotional condition and acknowledge any stress or anxiety you may be experiencing. By encouraging conscious awareness, this exercise helps you establish a relationship with your emotions.

**2. Deciphering Patterns to Find Triggers

Examine possible sources of your anxiousness. Make a note of any circumstances, ideas, or occurrences that appear to presage elevated worry. Finding patterns opens the door to understanding the underlying reasons of your worry and developing wise coping mechanisms.

**3. Writing Expressively: Liberating Your Mind

Express yourself through writing if you're feeling depressed. Let your ideas come to you as you write in your journal. This raw outpouring gives you a cathartic release and aids in the processing and externalization of your worry.

**4. Disrupt Negative Thoughts by Changing Your Viewpoint

As you write in your journal, confront any unfavorable ideas related to anxiousness. Examine other, more impartial viewpoints and consider challenging the veracity of these ideas. By encouraging cognitive restructuring, this technique gives you the ability to change your perspective.

**5. Journaling Gratitude: Fostering Positive Attitude

Include keeping a thankfulness journal in your routine. Consider the good things in your life to combat anxiety. No matter how little the act of gratitude, record it. This deliberate concentration on the positive can be a comforting salve for worried thoughts.

**6. Mindfulness Exercises: Grounding Yourself in the Present

Include periods of mindfulness throughout your writing. Give a detailed account of the sights, sounds, and textures you experienced. By practicing mindfulness and grounding yourself in the present, you can cultivate serenity and lessen the hold that anxiety has over you.

**7. Introspection: Dissecting Benevolent Feelings

Go deep into introspection in your journal. Examine the underlying feelings that are connected to anxiety. Are you currently feeling this way because of unresolved anxieties, concerns, or events from the past? Clarity and the facilitation of emotional processing result from deciphering these feelings.

**8. Creating Objectives for Coping Mechanisms: Strengthening Resilience

Establish attainable objectives for coping mechanisms. Decide on practical actions you can do in the event of anxiety. These objectives form your resilience toolkit and can include deep breathing, going for a little stroll, or asking for help.

**9. Monitoring Patterns of Anxiety: Raising Awareness

Create a mechanism for tracking patterns. Take note of how often, how strong, and how long your anxiety lasts. You may see trends with this tracking, which gives you useful information to comprehend your anxiety tendencies over time.

**10. Anxiety Affirmations: Building Strength

Incorporate anxiety-reduction-focused affirmations. Make affirmations that speak to you; for example, "I have the strength to manage my anxious thoughts" or "I am resilient in the face of anxiety." To strengthen a resilient and strong mindset, repeat these affirmations.

Imagine your anxiety diary as a compass that will lead you through the maze of emotions as you begin your adventure with it. Anxiety journaling becomes a transforming process through self-awareness, introspection, and deliberate practices; it becomes an alchemical realm where worries are transformed into wisdom and resilience grows in the rich soil of self-understanding.

4j:.Mindful Walking

Tromping With knowledge pilgrimaging With Intent Walking with mindfulness turns into a practice in living in time, a tardy perambulation where every step becomes a conscious note and the road becomes a oil for presence. Let's explore the fashion of aware walking as a way to cultivate mindfulness, serenity, and a more intimate connection with the natural world.

** 1. Creating a Vision Walking Towards Your ideal

Previous to beginning your aware walking program, set an ideal. relating your purpose allows you to designedly engage in every action, whether it's to enhance focus, cultivate inner serenity, or simply savor the present.

** 2. Breathing With mindfulness Matching Breath With Movement

Match your breathing to your walking style. Take a deep breath before each stride and release it gradually later. By coinciding your breathing with your movements, you can produce this metrical cotillion of mindfulness that helps you stay predicated on the present moment.

** 3. Perceiving Every Body Movement

Pay attention to the sensations that are passing in your body. Observe the slight variations in your weight as you lift and lower your bases. See how your body touches the ground, your arms swing smoothly, and your muscles contract. This increased body mindfulness makes walking further privately connected to you.

** 4. Observing Your surroundings Employing Your Senses

Come further conscious of the terrain around you. Observe the colors, shapes, and textures. Pay attention to the sounds each around you, including the howl of leaves, twittering catcalls, and far- out business. Using your senses in the moment enhances the uproarious ness of your aware walking experience.

** 5. Eye- opening Trampoline Contemplation

Include walking contemplation in your diurnal practice. Choose a focal point, similar as your breath, a mantra, or the sensation of each stride. When your studies wander, gently bring them back to the focal point you have chosen. Going on a walk while rehearsing awareness enhances attention.

** 6. Pace Awareness Chancing Your True Speed

Observe how snappily you walk. Whether your natural meter is calm and reflective or fast and brisk, pay attention to it. Move at a pace that aligns with your thing so that each step has purpose.

** 7. Developing ap reciativeness A Path to Gratitude

Keep gratefulness in mind as you move forward. Admit the blessing of your mobility and the sheer joy it brings. Cultivate an station of appreciativeness for the occasion to walk.

** 8. Conscious Transitions Embracing onsets and Ends

When you begin and end your aware perambulation, notice how your experience changes.

Gradationally turn your focus back from the practice to your surroundings. Making this conscious change will allow you to profit from awareness in other areas of your life.

** 9. Calm tromping Embracing Silence

Take a silent break during your thoughtful perambulation. Take remove any external distractions so that your movements come a peaceful symphony. As you move through the area, drink a sense of inner serenity and accept the silence.

** 10. Reflection and Gratitude Concluding Your Walk With mindfulness

After your walk with mindfulness, take a moment to reflect. Consider the perceptivity gained, the feelings endured, and the appreciation that grew. This silent contemplation period ends your aware walking experience.

With each stride, aware walking practice allows one to come a aware brushstroke, painting a picture of presence and connection. When you walk with purposeful mindfulness, the simple act of walking transforms into a profound trip where the fabric of aware life reveals the godliness of every step.

Chapter 5: Tools for Pain Management

The chapter on pain management methods unfolds as a caring guide in the fabric of emotional well-being, a set of techniques intended to help readers negotiate the complex terrain of both physical and emotional suffering. In order to promote resilience and well-being in the midst of suffering, this chapter invites you to investigate a toolset that encompasses holistic approaches.

5a..Template for a Pain Diary

Date: [Enter Date]**When is it?** (morning, afternoon, evening)

[**Location**: Where are you? Home/Office/Exterior]

Pain Level (1–10): On a scale of 1 to 10, with 10 being the most severe pain, indicate the degree of your discomfort.

Describe the bodily feelings you experience in relation to your pain. Is it painful, throbbing, dull, or sharp? Keep track of any variations in feeling during the day.

Trigger or Cause: Determine any possible sources of the pain. Was it because of a particular activity, stress, sleep deprivation, or something else entirely?

Engaging in:
Enumerate the things you did either prior to or during the pain. Incorporate mental and physical exercises.
Make a note of any mind-body strategies you used to control the discomfort, such as progressive muscle relaxation, deep breathing, or mindfulness.

Medication and Interventions: Keep track of any drugs you take and any pain management techniques you employ. Add the dosage and the efficacy.

Describe your current emotional condition. Are you experiencing any other feelings, such as relaxation, anxiety, or stress?

Sleep Quality: Evaluate how well you slept the previous evening. Add the hours that you slept as well.

Nutrition: Keep track of your snacks and meals. Make a note of any food decisions that might have affected your pain.

Social Interactions: Talk about any encounters with people or assistance you've had. Did interacting with people change how you felt about your pain?

Remarks/Observations:
Write down any further thoughts, observations, or revelations regarding your pain experience in this space.

Extra Advice

Consistency: To spot patterns and trends, consistently record your discomfort in the journal.

Honesty: To give a true picture of your pain experience, be truthful and thorough in your descriptions.

Triggers: Be aware of possible triggers and look for strategies to control or stay away from them.

Progress tracking: Keep a pain journal to monitor changes over time and evaluate how well pain management techniques are working.

Keeping a pain journal can help you better understand your pain, see trends, and work with medical specialists to customize your pain management strategy.

5b:Heat and Cold Therapy

Cooling and Heating Therapy: Calming the Senses

Heat and cold therapy are helpful friends in the field of pain management because they soothe sore muscles, reduce discomfort, and promote relief. Let's investigate the practice of heat and cold treatment as a complementary means of improving your overall health and calming your senses.

Heat Therapy: Accepting Cozy Coziness

1. Warm Cushion:

Put a warm compress on the injured region.

As the soothing warmth seeps into your muscles and encourages calm, experience it.

2. Bottle of Hot Water:

Warm, not hot, water should be put into a hot water bottle.

Apply it lightly to the desired location to provide a comforting hug.

3. Warm Shower:

Spend some time in a warm bath.

Let the comforting warmth diffuse your stress and encourage calm.

4. Warming Mat:

Turn the heating pad's temperature down to medium.

Feel the comforting heat as it relieves tense muscles.

5. A cozy shower

Take pleasure in a warm shower aimed at the injured area.
Let yourself feel relieved and at ease as the warmth cascades down.

Cold Therapy: Cooling Remedy

1. Chilled Bag:

On the afflicted area, use a cold pack or ice pack covered in a thin cloth.
Feel the cool, refreshing sensation as it helps to numb discomfort and reduce swelling.

2. Chilled Press:

Put some cold water on a cloth, wring it out, and apply it to the affected region.
Sensate yourself to the cool compress's soothing, organic alleviation.

3. Applying Ice:

After freezing water in a paper cup, remove the top and use the exposed ice to massage the affected area.
Savor the focused cooling for area-specific relief.

4. Cold Shower:

Place the impacted region in a basin filled with cold water.

Feel the revitalizing effect of cold water as it eases and lessens inflammation.

5. A chilly shower

Take a quick, cold shower to revitalize and revive yourself.

Let the refreshing water ease your stress and encourage awareness.

Success Suggestions:

Duration: Do not apply heat or cold for longer than fifteen to twenty minutes at a time.

Protection: When applying directly to your skin, use a thin towel to shield it.

Comfort: Determine the ideal temperature for your comfort and relaxation.

Consultation: Before utilizing heat or cold therapy, get advice from a healthcare provider if you currently have any health issues.

When you practice heat and cold treatment, picture it as a kind of gentle dance, where the movements of coldness and warmth combine to bring relaxation and comfort. Allow these therapies to become essential components of your pain relief arsenal, providing relief and enhancing overall well being.

5c:Gentle Exercise

Moderate Exercise: Embracing Movement for Overall Wellness
Gentle exercise becomes a compassionate practice in the context of pain management, a harmonious fusion of movement and mindfulness that nourishes your body and soul. Together, we will examine how to improve your flexibility, release stress, and cultivate a feeling of well-being through the practice of gentle exercise.

1. Strolling: An Introspective Walk
Take a leisurely stroll through a natural area. Inhale deeply, concentrate on each step, and relish the moment you have with your environment.

2. Do Yoga to Boost Flexibility

Examine calming yoga positions meant to increase your flexibility.

Accept the way the body is moving and let each pose develop with conscious awareness.

3. Tai Chi: Elegant Motion

Learn the peaceful martial art of tai chi, which emphasizes smooth and purposeful motions.

Discover the meditative aspect of Tai Chi, which encourages relaxation and balance.

4. Water: Effervescent Calm

Savor a swim in a body of water or a pool.

Experience the buoyancy of the water as it supports your motions, offering a mild yet efficient exercise.

5. Pilates to Strengthen Your Core

Include Pilates routines to build core strength.

Pay attention to deliberate motions that improve muscle balance and stability.

6.Cycling: Low-Impact Pleasure

Enjoy a leisurely bike ride while maintaining a steady and smooth pace.

Enjoy the pleasure of riding as a mind- and body-stirring, low-impact form of exercise.

**7. A Routine of Gentle Stretching

Set aside time for a mild stretching regimen. Concentrate on tense spots, progressively reducing constriction and encouraging suppleness.

**8. Chair Exercises: Movement While Seated.

Perform workouts meant to be done while seated. Examine mild exercises that increase blood flow and reduce stiffness; these are particularly advantageous for people who struggle with mobility.

**9. Qi Gong: Harmonizing Energy

Qi Gong is a traditional Chinese workout regimen that emphasizes movement and breathing. Gently, meditatively, glide through movements that cultivate harmony.

**10. Breathing Techniques for Mindfulness: Centering Breath

Incorporate attentive breathing exercises with mild activity.

Breathe in rhythm with every motion to generate a peaceful, flowing flow of energy and calm.

Success Suggestions:

Take Note of Your Body: Observe your body's reaction and modify the intensity as necessary.

Key to Consistency: Include mild exercise on a regular basis for long-term advantages.

Adjust as Necessary: Exercises can be modified to fit your comfort level and any physical restrictions.

Being Aware Mindfully: With each action, be alert and in the moment, paying attention to your breath and your senses.

When you do gentle exercise, picture it as a dance, a rhythmic fusion of movement and awareness that enhances your overall health. In your journey toward pain management, let each mild activity be a loving gesture to your body, one that enhances vitality, eases stress, and cultivates harmony.

5d: Pain Medication Management

Managing Painkillers: Striking a Balance Between Pain Relief and Wellness Being medicated can be a vital tool in the fight against pain, providing relief and enhancing overall health. Let's look at the skill of managing pain medications, which entails finding a careful balance between utilizing medications responsibly and prioritizing your general health.

**1. Consulting with a health care provider

Have a conversation with your healthcare provider. Discuss your medical background, the symptoms of your pain, and any preferences or concerns you may have regarding using medicines.

**2. Understanding Your Medication Options

Find out what kinds of painkillers are available. Understand the different types of painkillers, including analgesics, anti-inflammatory medications, and others.

**3. Customized Medication Plan

Make a personalized medication schedule with your healthcare provider.

Consider factors such as the type and intensity of your pain, any potential side effects, and your overall health.

**4. Medication Dosage and Schedule

Follow the prescription regimen your doctor has prescribed for you on a regular basis.

Do not alter the dosage on your own without first seeing a healthcare professional. Instead, adhere to the recommended instructions.

**5. Combining Therapies

Look at combination therapies, which may entail different types of painkillers.

Discuss the benefits and drawbacks of combining medications to get the most effective pain treatment.

**6. Remarks and Adjustments

Monitor the effectiveness of your drug on a frequent basis.

Notify your healthcare provider of any changes in your discomfort or side effects so they can adjust as needed.

**7. Managing Unfavorable Responses

Be aware of the potential side effects that taking your medication may cause.
Report any unfavorable reactions to your healthcare provider right away for guidance.

**8. Including the Pain Diary

When giving yourself your medication, make sure to include your pain journal.
Monitor your pain threshold, use of prescription drugs, and any connections in other aspects of your health.

**9. Communication with Medical Personnel

Maintain open channels of contact with your medical team.
Discuss any concerns, questions, or changes to your pain management needs.

**10. A Thorough Approach

Incorporate pain relievers into a holistic plan for general well-being.
Consider additional strategies such as physical activity, relaxation techniques, and lifestyle modifications.

Achievement Advice to Do:

Instruction: Understand the objectives, potential side effects, and combinations of the painkillers you take.

Adherence: Follow your prescription's instructions and take your medications as directed.

Lobbying: Participate actively in discussions with your healthcare provider to speak up for your health.

Frequently Occurs: Schedule regular meetings with your healthcare provider to go over and adjust your pain management strategy.

See the art of managing pain medication as a collaborative symphony—a harmonious combination of medications, communication with your healthcare team, and comprehensive approaches to health and well-being. By striking this careful balance, you can put your overall health and quality of life first while simultaneously giving yourself the tools you need to effectively manage pain.

5e: Mind-Body Practices

Mind- Body ways Harmony in Reconstruction
Mind- body conditioning crops as
transubstantiation tools in the pain operation
sanctuary, inviting a harmonious cotillion between
the body's wisdom and the mind's complexity.
Together, we will examine how to produce inner
calm, adaptability, and comprehensive well- being
via the art of mind- body conditioning.

** 1. Meditating to Develop Inner Calm

Accept the practice of contemplation as a way to
calm your studies. detect a comfortable spot, pay
attention to your breathing, and let ideas come and
go without attachment.

** 2. Exercises for Deep Breathing nutritional Breath

Practice deep breathing to ameliorate your capability
to relax. sluggishly exhale through your mouth after
taking a deep breath through your nose. Concentrate
on each breath cycle.

** 3. Gradational Pressure Release via Muscle Relaxation

To relieve physical pressure, engage in progressive muscle relaxation. Each muscle group should be totally tensed and also relaxed to encourage peace of mind and physical well- being.

** 4. Guided Imagery Comfort- converting Visualization

Try using guided imagery to take your mind to peaceful settings. Shut your eyes and let your studies wander to a serene position, seeing it easily.

** 5. Present- Moment Awareness in Mindfulness- Grounded Stress Reduction(MBSR)

Practice Stress Reduction Through awareness. Accept the present moment by engaging in aware eating, walking, and body checkup contemplations.

** 6. Biofeedback Awareness of the Mind- Body Connection

Make use of biofeedback ways to raise knowledge regarding the mind- body relationship. Get immediate feedback on your body's responses, giving you the control to manage your stress situations.

**** 7. Yoga Body- Mind Unification** Accept the holistic approach to yoga. To promote harmony between the body and the mind, flow through soft positions, attentive breathing, and contemplation.

**** 8. Autogenic Training Relaxation** Produced by Oneself Examine autogenic training to learn how to relax on your own. Make use of tone-suggestions to help you relax and feel better about yourself.

**** 9. Hypnotherapy Directed Calm** For guided relaxation and pain control, suppose about hypnotherapy. Take advantage of sessions led by a good therapist to discover the possible advantages of hypnotism.

**** 10. Moving Contemplation with Tai Chi**
Use Tai Chi as a form of movement contemplation. To ameliorate inflexibility, balance, and inner serenity, inflow via slow, purposeful movements.

Success Suggestions durability Constantly incorporate mind- body ways for accretive goods.

Adaptation Acclimate procedures to your preferences and degree of comfort.

Conscious Presence Embrace the experience to the fullest by approaching each exercise with an aware presence.

Self- Restraint Accept tone- compassion and admit that mind- body conditioning are a gradational, growing process as you move through them.

When you begin your trip with mind- body practices, picture it as a symphony, a beautiful commerce of movement, breath, and knowledge that waves a mending and well- being shade. By fostering this internal-physical bond, you give yourself the capability to deal with the complexity of pain in a graceful and flexible way.

5f: Distraction Techniques.

Distraction Strategies: Changing Attention, Relieving Stress

Distraction strategies are useful tools in the field of pain management because they allow you to change your focus, divert your attention from your agony, and discover brief periods of relief. Let's investigate the practice of distraction tactics as a dynamic way to move across the pain environment.

**1. Creative Escape Through Engaging Hobbies

Become engrossed in activities that hold your interest.

Creative endeavors, such as painting, writing, or playing an instrument, provide a satisfying way to unwind.

**2. Conscientious Coloring: Meditative Art

Examine coloring mindfully as a calming pastime. Open complex coloring books and let the rhythmic lines induce a meditative state.

**3. Harmony in Music: A Healing Experience

Make playlists with your favored calming tunes. Let the songs take you away and serve as a reassuring soundtrack for your day.

**4. Audiobooks and Podcasts: Cognitive Investigation

Listen to audiobooks or podcasts about subjects that interest you.

Take in engrossing stories to take your mind off of your hurt.

**5. Virtual Reality (VR) Diversion: Captivating Retreats

Examine uses for virtual reality that are intended to divert.

Take part in immersive activities that take you to tranquil settings or interactive journeys.

**6. Brain-Challenging Puzzle Games

Take pleasure in mentally stimulating puzzle games. Playing games like Sudoku or crosswords offers distraction and mental challenge.

**7. Virtual Tours or Nature Walks: Outdoor Discovery

Take leisurely strolls in the outdoors or experience virtual tours of beautiful scenery.

Take in the natural beauty of the surroundings, which will help you feel at ease.

**8. Laughter and Humor: Bringing Joy

Look for amusing content, such as comedies, stand-up comedy, or amusing videos.
Endorphins are released when we laugh, which provides a healthy and uplifting diversion.

**9. Meaningful Conversations and Social Connections

Make social connections with your family and friends.
Having meaningful interactions offers a positive and encouraging diversion.

**10. Aromatherapy or Tactile Activities as a Sensory Diversion

Investigate tactile hobbies and aromatherapy as sources of distraction for the senses.
Redirect your concentration by indulging your senses with soothing textures or enticing scents.

Success Suggestions:

Diversity To keep your distraction tactics productive, switch up your repertoire.

Customization: Select pursuits that fit your preferences and areas of interest.

Planned Pauses: Include diverting activities in your planned pauses to offer respite on a regular basis.

Conscious Presence: Using mindful present, approach each distraction method and give it your whole attention.

When you go through the art of distraction approaches, picture it as a mosaic: a dynamic arrangement of several activities that come together to form a relieving and diversionary tapestry.

By adopting these strategies, you give yourself the ability to pause for brief periods of time, change your perspective, and weave a story of wellbeing throughout your pain management process.

5g:Sleep Hygiene

Establishing Sleep Hygiene to Encourage
Comfortable Sleep
Sleep hygiene turns out to be a significant tool for
health, so make sure you set up routines and
decorate your environment to promote restful and
rejuvenating nights. Let's look at how to maintain
proper sleep hygiene to enhance your quality of
sleep and enhance your overall health.

**1. Consistent Sleep Pattern: Harmonious Daily Routine

Establish a regular sleep schedule by making a bed
reservation and getting up at the same time every
day.
Align your sleep schedule with your body's
circadian rhythm.

**2. Create a Calm Transition for Your Night Time Schedule

Establish a calming nighttime routine to help your
body recognize when it's time to unwind.
To help you relax, take up calming activities like
reading, gentle stretching, or music listening.

3. Improve Sleep Environment: Serene Hideaway

Ensure that your sleeping area is cozy and conducive to rest.

To create a tranquil sanctuary, turn down the lights, adjust the room's temperature, and obtain comfortable bedding.

4. Reduce Screen Time: Use Technology During Your Bedtime.

Reduce your screen usage by at least one hour.

The blue light that electronics emit may block the hormone melatonin, which encourages sleep.

5. Intentional Consumption: Timing and Choices

Steer clear of heavy meals just before bed.

Prior to going to bed, if you're hungry, have a small, healthful snack.

6. Limiting Stimulants: Take Caffeine and Nicotine Into Consideration

Cut back on your caffeine and nicotine intake in the hours before bed.

These stimulants may cause sleep cycles to be disturbed and hinder slumber.

**7. Regular Exercise: Relax and Recharge

Regular exercise is recommended, but try to get your workout in a few hours before bed.
While working out late at night can be exhilarating, exercise can also help you sleep better.

**8. Stress Reduction: Unwind and Calm Down

Make time in your routine for activities that aid in your nighttime relaxation.
Techniques to help calm the mind include basic yoga poses, deep breathing, and meditation.

9. Sleep Limit: Vigilant Sleeping

If you do take naps during the day, try to avoid taking them shortly before bed and limit how long you nap to twenty to thirty minutes.
Strategic napping can increase attentiveness without interfering with nighttime sleep.

**10. Comfort Is Crucial; Check Your Pillows and Mattress.

Check the comfort and support of your mattress and pillows.

Invest in bedding that is cozy and meets your preferences to guarantee a restful night's sleep.

Success Pointers:

Gradual Adjustments: Make little changes at first to give your body time to acclimate.

Typical Routine: Maintain a consistent sleep routine, even on the weekend.

Creating Connections: Establish a positive mental association with your sleeping area.

Conversation: Should you still be experiencing difficulties falling asleep, consult a healthcare professional for advice.

Imagine your healthy sleep habits as a well-balanced symphony of routines and behaviors that promote restful sleep and enhance your overall well-being.

By implementing these practices, you look after the foundation for healing sleep and allow each night to function as a gentle note in the harmony of your overall well being.

5h:Supportive Devices

Supportive Technology: Improving Comfort and Welfare

Supportive gadgets come into play as indispensable friends in the field of pain management since they are comfortable, facilitate mobility, and give users a sense of empowerment. Together, we will examine the art of supportive gadgets as adaptable instruments that improve your day-to-day functioning and augment your general welfare.

**1. Ergonomic Comfort in Orthopedic Pillows

Make use of orthopedic pillows that promote healthy spinal alignment.
Select pillows that offer customized comfort and fit your sleeping preferences.

**2. Ergonomic Seats: Support for Posture

Invest in posture-supporting ergonomic chairs.
These chairs ease tension and encourage proper spinal alignment at work or at home.

**3. Neck Support using Cervical Collars

To stabilize and support your neck, think about wearing a cervical collar.
Those who have neck injuries or pain may find these devices helpful.

4. Knee Braces: Stability of the Joint
To give the knee joint stability and support, use knee braces.
To choose the best type for your needs, speak with a healthcare practitioner.

5. Compression Sleeves: Improving Circulation
Accept compression sleeves for your arms and legs.
These sleeves can improve blood flow and offer assistance when exercising.

6. Carpal Tunnel Relief with Wrist Splints
Look into wrist splints for assistance in treating ailments such as carpal tunnel syndrome.
These gadgets can ease discomfort during wrist-training exercises.

7. Foot Comfort with Orthopedic Shoes
Choose supportive and comfortable orthopedic footwear.

These shoes can encourage good alignment and offer relief from foot ailments.

**8. Back Braces: Supporting Spine

For more spinal support, think about getting a back brace.

Those who are healing from injuries or who have back pain may find these gadgets useful.

**9. Mobility Aids: Strengthening of Independence

Examine walking sticks, crutches, and canes as mobility aids.

For people who struggle with movement, these gadgets support them and increase their independence.

**10. Custom Orthotics: Tailored Assistance

Obtain personalized orthotics to help with particular gait and foot problems.

Speak with a podiatrist to design inserts that are specific to your requirements.

Success Suggestions:

Professional Counseling: Consult medical experts for advice while choosing assistive technology.

Frequent Evaluation: Evaluate your devices' fit and efficacy on a regular basis.

Progressive Integration: Gradually introduce assistive equipment so that adjustments can be made.

Personalized Method: Select gadgets based on your own requirements and tastes.

When you learn to use supportive gadgets, think of them as trustworthy allies on your path to wellbeing. Every gadget has a distinct function that enhances your comfort, freedom of movement, and sense of empowerment. By incorporating these helpful resources into your everyday routine, you may compose a harmonious support system that improves your general comfort and deepens your understanding of pain management.

5i:Physical Therapy:Physical Therapy: Facilitating Mobility and Healing

Physical therapy is a cornerstone in the field of pain management. It is an empowering method that uses movement to improve general well-being, lessen suffering, and accelerate healing. Together, we will examine the practice of physical therapy as a transforming instrument for achieving optimal health.

****1. Thorough Evaluation:** Comprehending Your Requirements
Start with a thorough evaluation performed by a licensed physical therapist.
Determine problem areas, assess mobility, and together set individualized objectives.

****2. Specific Training Plans: Increasing Power and Agility
Participate in specialized workout regimes to address particular musculoskeletal problems.
Strengthening, increasing flexibility, and increasing general mobility are some goals of exercise.

3. Manual Therapy Approaches: Direct Assistance

Profit from the physical therapist's manual therapy procedures.

Soft tissue manipulation, joint mobilization, and massage are a few techniques that can help with pain management and better function.

4. Range-of-motion and stretching exercises: improving flexibility

Stretching and range-of-motion activities should be included to improve flexibility.

The purpose of these exercises is to loosen up and improve joint mobility.

5. Functional Movement Instruction: Practical Use

Take part in training with functional movements that mimics everyday tasks.

Using this method helps you do everyday chores more quickly and easily.

6. Posture Adjustment: Body Alignment

Utilize focused activities to address posture-related problems.

Encouraging good posture can help reduce pain and reduce strain on muscles.

**7. Exercises for Balance and Coordination: Strengthening Stability

Engage in activities that enhance your coordination and balance.

These exercises are essential for improving general stability and preventing falls.

**8. Coping Strategies for Pain Management

Discover pain management techniques suited to your individual requirements.

These could involve methods like stress management, breathing exercises, and mindfulness.

**9. Education and Changing Your Lifestyle: Providing Knowledge

Learn about your illness and how to take care of it. Examine lifestyle changes that support your long-term health objectives.

**10. At-Home Workout Plans: Maintaining Progress After Sessions

Use the at-home workout regimens that your physical therapist has prescribed.
Progress obtained during therapy sessions is reinforced when recommended activities are performed consistently at home.

Success Suggestions:

Transparent Communication Keep lines of communication open regarding your development and any worries you may have with your physical therapist.

Maintain consistency by following your doctor's workout regimens and showing up on time for therapy appointments.

Advocacy: Take an active role in your recovery process and speak out for your objectives and requirements.

Gradual Advancement: To reduce the chance of injury and prevent overexertion, increase the intensity of your workouts gradually.

Envision physical therapy as a dynamic journey where movement, rehabilitation, and empowerment are purposefully explorer as you immerse yourself in the art of physical therapy.

Working together with your physical therapist and accepting the customized strategies they offer, you build the fortitude and resiliency required to overcome the obstacles of pain and promote a peaceful coexistence of mobility and wellness in your life.

5j: Relaxation Techniques

Relaxation Methods: Maintaining Peace During the Storm

Relaxation techniques are gentle yet effective strategies for managing discomfort. They invite you to create a peaceful haven amidst life's obstacles. Let's investigate the practice of relaxation techniques as a means of promoting calmness on your path to wellbeing by calming your body and mind.

**1. Breathing Techniques: Taking Care of Your Breath

Practice deep breathing to lay the groundwork for calm.

With attention to each breath cycle, take a deep inhale with your nose, hold it for a while, and then gently release it through your mouth.

2. Gradual Tension Release via Muscle Relaxation

To relieve physical tension, engage in progressive muscle relaxation.

As you systematically contract and then release each muscle group, your body will experience a wave of calm.

3. Guided Visualization: Calm Imagery

Try using guided visualization to take your thoughts to serene settings.

Shut your eyes and visualize a peaceful scene in great detail. Let your thoughts stray into the peaceful realm.

4. Mindfulness-Based Meditation: Focusing on the Present

Take up mindfulness meditation to become more aware of the present moment.

To keep your consciousness anchored in the present now, pay attention to your breath, your sensations, or a guided meditation.

**5. Autogenic Training: Creating Calm on Your Own

To achieve self-generated relaxation, engage in autogenic training.

Self-suggestions might help you relax and feel better about yourself.

**6. Stretching and Yoga: Intentional Movement

Include some little stretching or yoga in your regimen.

Permit the rhythmic flow of motions to encourage mental and physical calm.

**7. Aromatherapy: Calm Aromas

Try aromatherapy with soothing smells like chamomile or lavender.

Create a sensory oasis by taking in the calming scents.

**8. Therapeutic Harmony Through Music Listening

Create relaxing music playlists.
Let the music wash over you, offering a peaceful background for your downtime.

**9. Stimulating Meditation with Mindful Walking

As a kind of moving meditation, engage in mindful walking.
When you walk, use all of your senses to create a strong bond between your body and mind.

**10. Water Therapy in a Hot Bath or Shower

To help your muscles relax, treat yourself to a hot bath or shower.
Let the warm water wrap you in a cocoon of calm as you submerge yourself in it.

Success Suggestions:

Continual Application: For ongoing advantages, include relaxation techniques into your everyday practice.

Customization: Investigate many methods to determine which one most appeals to you.

Silent Setting: Establish a calm, cozy area for your relaxation exercises.

Frequent Arrivals: Regular self-checks are a good way to gauge how stressed you are and how well your relaxation methods are working.

When you practice relaxation techniques, picture them as a gentle breeze—a calming force that dissipates stress, fosters serenity, and carves out a tranquil haven on the canvas of your life. By introducing these practices into your daily routine, you invite moments of calm that enhance your general state of well-being and fortitude in the face of life's challenges.

Chapter 6: Stress-Reduction Tools:

Managing Life's Unpredictable Seas

Greetings and welcome to a chapter devoted to the skill of navigating the rough waters of stress. We'll discover stress-reduction strategies that are customized for your day-to-day existence in this investigation—a compass to help you navigate the ups and downs and find moments of peace amid life's obstacles.

6a: River of Life: Time Management Techniques for Stress Adjustment

Good time management makes you a resilient vessel amid life's fast-moving currents, enabling you to handle stress. In order to withstand the stress storms, let's delve deeper into the tactics and untangle the productivity and balance sails.

**1. Setting Priorities: Utilizing Your Compass

Set priorities for your duties based on their effect on your wellbeing as well as their urgency.
Make sure the things on your to-do list are in line with your values and will help you achieve your long-term objectives and happiness.

**2. Scheduling Your Time: Creating Your Program

Extend time blocking to include leisure and self-care activities in addition to work-related chords.
Set aside specified time slots for hobbies, leisure, and soul-stirring pursuits.

**3. To-Do Lists: Getting Things Done

Turn your to-do lists into deliberate stress-reduction roadmaps.
Incorporate self-care products with work-related responsibilities to create a well-rounded and intentional day.

**4. Make SMART goals: Well-being anchors

Integrate a wellness viewpoint into your SMART objectives.

Set objectives that will support your career development while also promoting your mental and emotional well-being.

**5. Streamlining for Serenity using Batch Processing

Use batch processing for enjoyable hobbies as well as work-related duties.

Combine self-care tasks to provide peaceful moments throughout the day.

**6. Minimize Multitasking: Appreciating the Trip

Remind yourself of the value of every minute by avoiding multitasking.

Give your whole attention to the work at hand, enjoying the ride rather than hurrying to get there.

**7. Time Audits: Taking Stock Among the Rushes

Utilize time audits for stress awareness as well as efficiency.

Examine how the way you spend your time affects your stress levels and modify your plan of action accordingly.

**8. Make Use of Technology: Traveling Allies

Use technology to your advantage as a travel companion for stress resilience.
Make notes about pauses, mindfulness exercises, and even when to check in with your emotional health.

**9. Effective Communication: Getting Along with Others

Be honest in your communication regarding your stress levels and time limits.
Encourage a cooperative atmosphere where people can relate to and support your dedication to stress-resilient time management.

**10. Vacations for Self-Care: Havens of Restoration

Transform self-care intervals from rest periods into havens of recuperation.

Take part in things that will actually give you more energy so you can tackle the problems that lie ahead.

Some Advice for Stress-Resistant Scheduling:

Moderate Modifications: When you modify your time management techniques to lessen stress, remember to treat yourself with kindness.

Appreciate small victories: Celebrate your development and give yourself credit for little victories and accomplishments along the way.

Regularly Evaluate: Review your time management techniques frequently to make sure they still meet your demands as they change.

Conscientious Shifts: When shifting between tasks, incorporate brief mindfulness exercises to help you stay relaxed.

Imagine these time management techniques as a well-made compass that will help you navigate the uncertain waters of life as you use them to manage stress. You can empower yourself to navigate through stress with resilience, aware of the currents yet grounded in a sense of balance and well-being, by incorporating these strategies into your daily journey.

6b:Mindfulness-Based Stress Reduction (MBSR

Taking Roots in the Present
Take a trip towards grounded calm by using Mindfulness-Based Stress Reduction (MBSR). This chapter will examine the life-changing discipline of mindfulness, which is a skill that allows you to deeply connect with the present moment while navigating the waves of stress.

1. Conscious Breathing: Using Your Breath as an Anchor
Start your mindful breathing adventure with MBSR. Utilizing each breath as a firm anchor to the here and now, focus your attention on it.

2. Examining the Interior Landscape with Body Scan Meditation
Practice body scan meditation to develop an awareness of your physical senses.

As you gradually turn your attention from head to toe, acknowledge and let go of any stress.

3. Meditation on Loving-Kindness: Fostering Compassion

In order to develop compassion, practice loving-kindness meditation.
Send positive vibes to both yourself and other people to create a cozy and intimate atmosphere.

4. Intense Stroking: Strolling Meditation

Make strolling a conscious activity.
Experience every stride, the flow of your movement, and the ground's hold on your body.

5. Awakening the Senses through Sensory Awareness

Practice sensory awareness to improve your perception.
Examine the abundance of the current moment's sights, sounds, tastes, smells, and textures.

6. Intentional Dining: Appreciating Every Bite

Engage in mindful eating to strengthen your bond with food.

Enjoy every meal, taking in the tastes, textures, and feeling of providing nourishment for your body.

7. Mind-Body Link: Comprehensive Understanding

Encourage a body-mind connection that is comprehensive by practicing mindfulness.

Acknowledge the interaction of thoughts, feelings, and bodily experiences.

8. Breath Awareness in Everyday Life: Convenient Calm

Incorporate breath awareness into your everyday routine.

Use your breath as a transportable anchor to the present, whether you're feeling happy or stressed.

9. Conscious Communication: Being Present During Conversation

Use mindfulness when conversing.

Engage in mindful speech, listen intently, and practice being present when interacting with others.

**10. Resources and Apps for Mindfulness:

Assisted Assistance
For guided support, look into mindfulness applications and tools.
These resources include organized practices and sessions to improve your MBSR experience.

Advice for Conscious Navigation:

Start Modestly Start out with short sessions and as you get more comfortable, gradually increase the length.

Continuity: For best results, include mindfulness exercises into your daily routine on a regular basis.

Non-Judgemental Remark: By observing your thoughts and feelings objectively, you can cultivate self-compassion.

Conscientious Shifts: For a smooth transition from one task to the next, incorporate meditative moments into your day.
When you start the MBSR path, picture mindfulness as a lighthouse: a beacon that guides you through the present moment, providing calm and clarity among the stressors. Engaging in these activities on

a regular basis helps you develop a strong connection with the richness of each moment, creating a strong anchor that keeps you rooted in the here and now and gives you the ability to handle stress with grace and awareness.

6c..Healthy Coping Mechanisms:

Effective Coping Techniques: Developing Storm-Resilience
In the fabric of life, effective coping mechanisms offer a strong and robust thread that offers consolation and strength in the face of difficulty. Now let's dive into this final chapter and discover how to use stress-reduction strategies to foster well-being and strengthen the foundation of inner resilience.

**1. Practice: Awakening the Spirit

Engage in physical activities you find enjoyable. Exercise becomes a useful tool for lowering stress and improving mood, whether it be yoga, dance, or brisk walking.

2. Creative Expression Unleashed: Imagination

Explore your artistic side in painting, writing, and music.
Expressing emotions creatively allows for a cathartic release and promotes self-discovery.

3. Nature Link: Finding Comfort in the Wide Open Spaces

Spend some time unwinding in the beautiful outdoors.
Whether you're strolling through a park or hiking in the mountains, the natural world offers a tranquil sanctuary.

4. Activities for Mindfulness: Locating Your Center

Embrace awareness outside of formal meditation sessions.
Incorporate mindfulness into your daily activities to cultivate a present-oriented and concentrated mentality.

5. Social Media Connections: Building a Support System

Foster close ties with the people you care about. Asking loved ones for support and sharing your experiences with them can help you become more emotionally resilient.

**6. Humor and Laughter: A Joyful Interlude

Create a humorous sense of humor as a coping mechanism.
Laughing provides momentary solace and supports a positive outlook.

**7. Restorative Sleep: Restoring the Mind

Prioritize obtaining adequate sleep in order to enhance overall health.
Create a calming evening routine and create a tranquil environment in your house for restful sleep.

**8. A Healthful Diet: Energizing the Body and Mind

Consume healthful, balanced meals to fuel your body.
An optimal nourished body fosters resilience and optimal cognitive function.

**9. Journaling as a Reflective Release

Maintain a journal as a tool for self-analysis. You can express yourself and practice introspection in a more tangible way by putting your thoughts and feelings down on paper.

**10. Methods of Breathing: Calming the Inner Fury

Include intentional breathing techniques in your daily routine. Breathing deeply and deliberately can help to calm the inner storm during stressful situations.

Tips for Increasing Resilience:

Moderation as opposed to Intensity The impact of using coping mechanisms consistently is higher than that of making forceful but sporadic attempts.

Customization: Modify your coping strategies to fit your unique needs and preferences.

Continual Integration: Introduce new coping strategies gradually to give yourself time to become used to them and incorporate them.

Self-Restraint: Acknowledge that improvement comes gradually and approach the process of developing resilience with empathy for yourself. Consider these constructive coping mechanisms as a tapestry, a collection of actions that work in unison to enhance your resilience and general well-being. By incorporating these into your everyday routine, you establish a stronghold that empowers you to weather stress-related storms with a resilient heart and a renewed sense of vitality.

6d:Setting Boundaries Establishing Limits to Protect Your Well-Being

Greetings and welcome to a chapter devoted to the practice of boundary-setting, a crucial ability that protects your health and fosters a balanced, peaceful life. Let's examine how boundaries may change your life and help you handle the ups and downs of obligations with grace and resiliency.

1. Introspection: Recognizing Your Needs
To start, think on yourself and determine your requirements and priorities.

Recognize the aspects of your life where establishing limits will benefit your general wellbeing.

2. Unambiguous Communication: Expressing Your Boundaries

When expressing your boundaries, communicate in a straightforward and confident manner.
Make sure that everyone understands your wants and expectations by clearly stating your limitations.

3. Prioritization: Emphasizing What's Important

Set priorities for the important jobs and obligations you have.
Decide what is most important to you so that you may spend your time and energy wisely.

4. Establish Your Capacity and Learn to Say No

Accept the ability to say no when it's required.
Respect your limits and acknowledge that turning down requests is a legitimate and essential kind of self-care.

5. Set Work-Life Boundaries: Juggling Personal and Professional Life
Define distinct boundaries for your personal and professional lives.
Set apart specified periods of time for work and play to avoid letting work-related stress interfere with your personal life.

6. Technology Limitations: Disconnecting for Restorative Effects
Set restrictions on the usage of technology.
Set aside certain periods to disconnect from emails, messages, and alerts in order to make time for mental renewal.

7. Social Boundaries: Fostering Positive Relationships
Establish social boundaries to promote wholesome partnerships.
In order to sustain relationships and protect your wellbeing, be sure to express your requirements to others.

8. Time Management: Establishing Reasonable Goals

Make use of efficient time management techniques to establish reasonable goals.

****9. Consistent Reinforcement:** Maintaining Boundaries Evaluate your availability and capability before committing to assignments or engagements to avoid over committing.
Reinforce your boundaries consistently.
Determine and modify your boundaries on a regular basis in response to shifting priorities and conditions.

****10. Setting Boundaries for Self-Care: Giving Your Health Priority**
Acknowledge self-care as an essential boundary.
Make self-care routines a priority in order to support your physical, mental, and emotional well.

Boundary-setting advice:
Start Modestly Prioritize more difficult areas of your life by first establishing boundaries in the simpler ones.

Seek Assistance: Talk to people about your boundaries and ask for their support and understanding.

Flexibility: Recognize that your boundaries may change over time and be willing to make necessary adjustments.

Self-Advocacy: Be a confident advocate for yourself, understanding that establishing boundaries is a step toward personal strength.

Think of establishing boundaries as building a shield to protect you from life's demands; a shield that respects your needs, conserves your energy, and creates an environment in which you may respond to them with resilience and clarity. By incorporating this ability into your daily life, you build a foundation of wellbeing that enables you to deal with life's challenges with equilibrium and confidence.

6e..Humor and Laughter: A Happy Diversion from the Storm

Laughter and humor are like bright notes amid a symphony of tension, creating a melody of happiness and lightness. This chapter will examine the transforming power of laughing, which is a diversion that not only lifts the soul but also acts as a buoyant vessel over life's problems. Let's get started.

The Essence of Laughter: Laughter is a universal language that cuts across barriers because of its contagious and liberating nature. It is an impromptu display of happiness that possesses the amazing power to release stress and foster a sense of mutual satisfaction. Accepting humor in our lives turns it into an art form, a means of elevating the ordinary to the spectacular.

1. The Healing Power of Laughter: Laughing has real healing benefits; it's not just a fleeting diversion.
Laughter physiologically releases endorphins, which enhance happiness and can even momentarily reduce pain.

2. Developing a Humorous Perspective: Use a humorous viewpoint to help you see the difficulties in life.
Discovering the comedy in trying circumstances can give you a new perspective and help problems appear more double.

3. Laughter Yoga and Exercises: Try out some exercises and laughter yoga that encourage deliberate laughing.
For a boost of happiness, try laughing yoga or adding fun workouts to your program.

4. Comedy and Entertainment: Incorporate humor and amusement into your free time pursuits. Let laughing be a purposeful component of your pleasure, whether it's at a live performance, a comedy film, or a stand-up special.

5. Shared Laughter: Foster moments of laughter with family, friends, and other loved ones. Laughing together strengthens bonds and promotes a spirit of unity and happiness.

6. Playfulness in regular Life: Include a little playfulness in each of your regular activities. Have a playful approach when taking on work, finding delight and inventiveness in even the most basic endeavors.

****7. Laughing as a Stress Reliever:** Laughing is a powerful way to release stress.
When things get stressful, make a conscious effort to find the funny or do things that make people laugh out loud.

****8. Humorous Reflection:** Bring lighthearted reflection to difficult situations.
Once you have successfully navigated a stressful circumstance, consider it humorously, acknowledging its absurdity or opportunity for development.

****9. Laughing and Mindfulness:** Include laughing in your exercises involving mindfulness. Laughing mindfully promotes being totally present in the moment and lets happiness come to you naturally.

****10. Making a Humor Jar:** Create a "Humor Jar" in which you store amusing tales, proverbs, or incidents.
When you're feeling down, go back and read these gems for a quick laugh.

Suggestions for Creating Humor:

Let Go of Perfectionism Accept flaws in yourself and discover the humor in life's oddities.

Have fun: Embrace a lively mindset that lets joy and spontaneity come through.

Laughter Breaks: Throughout the day, especially during hectic or stressful times, schedule brief moments of laughter.

Tell Off Your Jokes: Tell those you know jokes, hilarious anecdotes, or interesting insights.
Think of them as bright, cheery balloons when it comes to humor and laughing. In addition to lifting your own spirits, deliberately including laughing in your life has a contagious impact that makes people around you happy.
 Let laughter be your comrade as you sail the seas of stress, providing you with a lovely sail that will carry you through the waves with resilience and an infectious enthusiasm for life.

6f:Exposure to Nature

Exposure to Nature: Reestablishing Calm

Enter the soothing embrace of nature, where the sound of rustling leaves, the soft murmur of a brook, and the wide-open spaces of foliage serve as a peaceful backdrop. This chapter will discuss the revitalizing benefits of spending time in nature—an immersive experience that calms the spirit and serves as a haven from the daily grind.

1. Nature's Healing Touch: The natural world has the innate capacity to mend and replenish. Stress reduction, mood enhancement, and an overall increase in well-being have all been related to exposure to natural areas.

2. Forest Bathing (Shinrin-Yoku): Take part in the Japanese tradition of forest bathing, often referred to as Shinrin-Yoku.
Take a leisurely stroll in a forest, using all of your senses to fully immerse yourself in the environment.

3. Outside Meditation: Take advantage of outdoor meditation to combine exposure to nature with awareness.
Locate a quiet area outside—a park, a garden, or your backyard—and practice mindful meditation there.

4. Nature Retreats & Getaways: Arrange regular trips or retreat into the natural world.
A day at the beach, a weekend camping trip, or a climb in the mountains—these activities provide a significant diversion from the ordinary.

5. Green Areas in Urban Settings: Look for green areas in urban settings.
Natural aspects can be included into your daily life through city parks, botanical gardens, or even a potted plant on your desk.

6. Naturalist-Inspired Activities: Take part in naturalist-inspired activities.
Engaging in activities such as gardening, birdwatching, or cloud gazing can foster a sense of connection with the natural world.

7. Sunlight and Vitamin D: Bask in their respective advantages.
To take advantage of the mood-enhancing properties of sunlight, spend time outside, especially during the day.

8. Nature Soundscapes: Construct or take in sounds of the natural world.
These auditory experiences—such as the sound of breaking waves, birdsong, or a light breeze—bring the peaceful spirit of nature indoors.

9. Outdoor Exercise: Incorporate physical activities with exposure to nature.
Engage in outdoor physical activities such as hiking, jogging, or yoga in a park to enhance your overall health and well-being.

10. Observing Nature With Mindfulness:
Engage in conscious observation of nature.
Spend some time silently studying the minutiae found in nature, such as the elaborate webwork of a spider or the patterns found in the leaves or flowers.

Advice for Loving the Outdoors:

Nature Breaks Every Day: Make time each day for quick excursions into nature, even if it's simply a quick walk at a local park.

Unplugged Nature Time: To completely immerse yourself in the experience, unplug all electronics during your time in nature.

Seasonal Exploration: Discover nature in various climates and settings as the seasons change.

Journaling outdoors: When you go outside, write down your observations, feelings, and thoughts in a nature journal.

Think of spending time in nature as a trip back to your origins—an investigation that reawakens your connection to the ageless cycles of the natural world. Let nature become a tapestry of tranquility as you incorporate it into your life; a haven where tension melts and a profound sense of peace arises.

6g: Hobbies and Leisure Activities

Embark on a delightful exploration of hobbies and leisure activities—a realm where passion meets play, and the pursuit of joy becomes a cherished journey. In this chapter, we'll unravel the profound impact that engaging in activities you love has on stress reduction and overall well-being.

**1. The Power of Pleasure:

Hobbies and leisure activities are not mere pastimes; they are powerful agents of pleasure.
Engaging in activities that bring joy stimulates the release of endorphins, contributing to a positive mood.

2. Discovering Personal Passions:

Take time to discover your personal passions and interests.
Whether it's painting, cooking, playing an instrument, or gardening, explore activities that resonate with your soul.

3. Mindful Engagement:

Approach your hobbies with mindfulness.
Immerse yourself fully in the activity, savoring each moment and letting go of stressors.

4. Creative Expression:

Use hobbies as a means of creative expression.
Whether through writing, drawing, or crafting, express your thoughts and emotions in a way that feels authentic to you.

5. Social Hobbies:

Embrace social hobbies that foster connections.

Join clubs, classes, or groups centered around your interests, creating opportunities for shared joy.

**6. Digital Detox through Hobbies:

Use hobbies as a form of digital detox.
Step away from screens and immerse yourself in offline activities, allowing your mind to unwind.

**7. Stress-Relieving Hobbies:

Seek out hobbies with inherent stress-relieving qualities.
Activities like gardening, knitting, or puzzles provide a meditative space that soothes the mind.

**8. Balancing Work and Play:

Create a balance between work and leisure.
Allocate dedicated time for hobbies, treating them as essential appointments for your well-being.

**9. Learning and Growth:

Choose hobbies that offer opportunities for learning and growth.
Whether acquiring a new skill or delving into a subject of interest, the journey itself becomes enriching.

****10. Seasons and Weather-Inspired Hobbies:**
Embrace hobbies that align with seasons and weather conditions.
Adjust your activities to match the changing atmosphere, connecting with nature's rhythms.

Tips for Joyful Pursuits:

Mix of Solo and Social Hobbies: Include both solo and social hobbies to cater for different aspects of your well-being.

Regular "Me Time": Schedule regular "me time" for your hobbies to ensure consistent self-care.

Experimentation: Be open to trying new hobbies, allowing for spontaneity and discovery.

Celebrate Progress: Celebrate your progress and achievements in your hobbies, no matter how small. Imagine hobbies and leisure activities as portals to joy—a collection of doorways that lead to moments of fulfillment and respite. As you infuse your life with these pursuits, let them become threads in the tapestry of your well-being—a vibrant mosaic that radiates joy and enriches the canvas of your daily existence.

6h:Social Support Networks

Social Support Systems: Foundations of Fortitude
Accept and appreciate social networks, which are
essential to the structure of resilience and mental
health. This chapter delves into the significant
influence of cultivating relationships, creating a web
of bonds that not only support you during difficult
times but also honor the wonder of life's common
experiences.

1. The Power of Connection: Social support
networks serve as the cornerstone for human
connection, which is a basic human need.
Emotional stability and a sense of belonging are
enhanced by the development of meaningful
relationships.

2. Diverse Support Networks: Encourage a
range of support networks that cover different facets
of your life.
These networks could include friends, family,
coworkers, and neighborhood associations; each

group can provide a different viewpoint and source of assistance.

3. Honest and Open Communication: Give honest and open communication top priority in your relationships.
Active listening and expressing thoughts and feelings promote understanding and deepen relationships.

4. Quality above Quantity: Give more weight to the caliber of your relationships than the number. A large but shallow social circle has less of an impact on well-being than meaningful, supporting interactions.

5. Reciprocity in Support: Promote mutual support among members of your social circles. Being both a supporter and a recipient of help fosters a balanced dynamic that strengthens the network as a whole.

6. Crisis Response Plans: Work with your support systems to create crisis response plans.

Having crisis management procedures and open lines of communication in place helps people feel secure when things go tough.

7. Social Rituals and Traditions: Make use of social customs and rituals in your interpersonal interactions.
Your social support network's ties are strengthened and a sense of continuity is created by these shared experiences.

8. Welcome to Virtual Support Communities: Take advantage of these online resources.
Online communities and forums can offer a useful setting for interacting with people who share similar struggles or experiences.

9. The Ability to Resolve Conflicts:
Develop your ability to resolve conflicts in interpersonal relationships.
Resolving disagreements amicably and constructively makes your social support system more resilient.

10. Celebrate Milestones: Join together to commemorate accomplishments and milestones.

A friendly and upbeat environment is reinforced when people acknowledge and celebrate each other's accomplishments.

Suggestions for Developing Social Support Systems:

Frequent Visits: To keep in touch, plan frequent check-ins with important members of your support system.

Manifest Your Thanks: Encourage a culture of appreciation by expressing your gratitude for the assistance you get.

Be Present: Make a point of paying close attention to conversations and being really present while valuing the connection.

Promote Vulnerability: Foster an atmosphere that values vulnerability to foster closer relationships. Think of your social support system like a garden: a rich environment with deep roots that fosters relationships. Let this garden become a haven that supports your mental health as you give it loving attention, offering comfort, happiness, and a voyage through life's journey together.

6i:Relaxation techniques

Explore the peaceful world of relaxation techniques, which are a symphony of methods that balance the body, mind, and spirit. We'll go into the art of relaxation in this chapter, giving you a variety of strategies to develop a profound sense of calm in the face of life's challenges.

1. Breathwork and Deep Breathing: As a basis for relaxation, start with breathwork.
Practice deep breathing techniques to help you stay focused and in a peaceful state of mind.

2. Progressive Muscle Relaxation (PMR):
To relieve stress, adopt Progressive Muscle Relaxation (PMR).
Different muscle groups should be systematically stiff and then relaxed to produce a feeling of physical and mental calm.

3. Guided vision and Imagery: Immerse yourself in the realm of guided vision and imagery. Allow your thoughts to create a peaceful and optimistic mental spaces by visualizing tranquil scenes or landscapes.

****4. Mindfulness Meditation**: Use this technique to cultivate present-moment awareness.
In order to develop a calm and focused state, pay attention to your breath, your body's feelings, or a particular point of interest.

****5. Body Scan Meditation**: Take a look at this method of meditation.
From head to toe, do a body scan, focusing on and releasing tension in each place.

****6. Learn about Autogenic Training:** This relaxation technique uses self-suggestions.
Employ words to encourage a state of calm by inducing both mental and physical relaxation.

****7. Yoga and Tai Chi:** Practices like yoga and tai chi should be followed.
These mindful movement techniques promote flexibility and relaxation by combining breath with light physical exertion.

****8. Aromatherapy and Essential Oils:**
Discover how these two complementary therapies might help you relax.
Scents that are recognized to promote relaxation include eucalyptus, lavender, and chamomile.

****9. Music and Calm Sounds**: To create a calming atmosphere, play some music and play some soothing sounds.
White noise, ambient sounds, or instrumental music can all improve your ability to unwind.

****10. Hydrotherapy and Hot Baths:** Include hydrotherapy or hot baths in your daily regimen for relaxation.
Warm water has the power to ease tense muscles and create a peaceful atmosphere that promotes mental rest.

Advice for Including Relaxation Methods:
Continuity: To get the most out of relaxation techniques, practice them frequently.

Establish a Calm Space: Set up a dedicated area that is distraction-free for relaxation.

Combine Methods: Try blending various relaxation methods to develop a customized, effective relaxation regimen.

Mindful Transitions: To encourage a sense of balance when switching between tasks, use relaxation techniques.

Think of relaxation techniques as soothing waves that flow in a rhythmic manner, relieving tension and bringing about a peaceful peacefulness. As you experiment and incorporate these techniques into your life, allow them to become a calming melody that leads you to a state of profound rest and renewal.

Chapter 7: Building Resilience

Fortifying Yourself Against Misfortune
In the intricate web of life, resilience is a fundamental strength that gives one the ability to surmount challenges and emerge stronger. This chapter takes the reader on a journey through the process of gaining resilience, which comprises learning from adversity and using it as an opportunity to further one's own development.

7a.. Embracing Change: Putting Your Trust in Life's Flow

Change is the sole constant in the enormous fabric of existence. This chapter explores the core discipline of accepting change. It's a call to embrace life's ups and downs and acknowledge that change is an essential part of what it is to be human.

The Dance of Impermanence: Change is a constant in life, much like in a dance, where each step leads to growth and advancement. We'll investigate the concept of impermanence and learn how the changing of the seasons affects our circumstances.

Navigate unexplored Seas: Accepting change is similar to venturing into unexplored terrain. We'll discuss the emotions we experience when we are in the unknown and how embracing change may transform our lives by giving us the courage and grace to face uncertainty head-on.

Release and Renewal: A common feature of change is letting go of the old to make room for the new. We'll discuss the art of release, understanding that letting go creates space for growth, rebirth, and unexpected chances to arise.

Creating a Flexible mindset: This chapter offers suggestions for creating a flexible and adaptive mindset. By altering our perspective on change, we can go from resistance to acceptance and welcome the opportunity for development and learning.

Finding Stability in the Face of Change: Despite the fact that change is unavoidable, stability can be found inside. We'll examine strategies and frames of view that support us in remaining grounded during trying times and preserving our resilience as we traverse the always shifting landscape of life.

Accepting Changes: Life is a series of transitions, each offering a chance for growth and a unique lesson. We'll discuss how embracing change helps us to embrace each new phase of life with curiosity and openness, whether it's in our careers or at personal milestones.

The Wisdom of Surrender: It is related to accept changes to be wise to surrender. We will discuss the importance of letting go of control, the freedom that comes with letting life unfold on its own timetable, and the value of surrendering control.

In the Midst of Change: Mindfulness turns into a dependable ally when things are changing. We'll examine how living in the present moment fosters tranquility and clarity, empowering us to handle change with poise.

Resilience in Change: When things change, one's resilience may be put to the test. We'll discuss how developing resilience in the midst of change involves adjusting, conquering challenges, and finding strength in the face of uncertainty.

The Beauty of the Unfolding Journey:
As we get to the end of our investigation, think of change not as a disruption but as a beautiful unfolding journey. Each twist and turn contributes a fragment to the puzzle that is our existence. A summons to fully participate in this amazing symphony of life is to accept change.

Let's welcome change, get the insight to recognize the beauty in every transition moment, and muster the courage to face the unknown.

7b:Adaptive Thinking

Adaptive Thinking: Handling Difficulties with a Strong Mind
Explore the world of adaptive thinking, a cognitive compass that enables us to navigate life's intricacies with adaptability, resilience, and the ability to flourish in the face of adversity. This chapter delves

into the practice of developing adaptable thinking as a potent means of improving mental health.

Comprehending Adaptive Thinking:
Essentially, adaptive thinking is a flexible cognitive process that enables us to modify our viewpoints and reactions in reaction to evolving situations. We'll explore the fundamentals of adaptable thinking and see how it helps us to deal with life's unpredictability.

Flexibility in Thought Patterns: This chapter provides guidance on how to encourage thought patterns to be more flexible. We may liberate ourselves from inflexible mental frames and tackle problems with a creative and adaptive mentality by developing an openness to divergent points of view and embracing ambiguity.

Adaptive thinking entails seeing setbacks as opportunities for personal development. We'll look at how viewing failures as teaching moments improves our capacity for recovery and builds resilience and fortitude.

Solution-Oriented Approaches:

An adaptable thinker takes a problem-solving approach to problems. We'll talk about how concentrating on doable fixes rather than wallowing in issues can result in efficient problem-solving and a proactive attitude toward the difficulties of life.

Accepting Change as a Catalyst: Although change is frequently seen as disruptive, it can really be welcomed as an engine for development. We'll look at how adopting an adaptive mindset enables us to accept change as a chance for growth and see it as a normal and transforming part of the journey.

Cognitive Restructuring: This chapter explores the idea of cognitive restructuring, which is recognizing and confronting unfavorable thought processes. We may cultivate a more adaptive and happy attitude and enhance emotional wellbeing by changing the way we think.

Thinking with Mindfulness: Adaptive thinking is built on mindfulness. We will talk about how developing mindful awareness helps us to observe our ideas objectively, which promotes a present-centered, nonjudgmental approach to cognitive processes.

Developing Emotional Control: Emotional control and adaptive thinking go hand in hand. We'll look at methods for identifying and controlling our emotions so that we can face difficulties head-on and act coolly under pressure.

The Function of Self-Compassion: In adaptive thinking, self-compassion serves as a compass. We'll talk about how being kind and empathetic to ourselves when things get tough improves our capacity for adaptation and builds resilience and inner strength.

Creating an Adaptive Thinking toolbox: To sum up, think of adaptive thinking as a cognitive toolbox that helps you deal with life's curveball. Every technique, from mindfulness exercises to reframing techniques, aids in the growth of an adaptable and robust mind.

Adaptive thinking appears as a thread that ties obstacles together to create a fabric of growth and resilience in the emotional well being tapestry. May the study of adaptable thinking serve as a beacon for you, showing the way to a stronger, more vibrant mind as you go deeper into its inquiry.

7c: Learning from Setbacks

Acknowledging Failures as a Foundation for Personal Development
In life's symphony, obstacles frequently perform a difficult yet transforming theme. This investigation into the art of learning from failures is an invitation to not only persevere through hardship but also to extract insightful knowledge that can promote resilience and personal development.

Reinterpreting Failures as Chances:
Failures are not the end, but rather a turning point toward improvement. We'll explore the skill of rephrasing failures such that we see them as opportunities rather than as tragedies. Accepting this way of thinking enables us to gain insightful knowledge despite hardship.

Resilience in the Face of Difficulties:
Recognizing that obstacles are a necessary part of life, we investigate the development of resilience.

Through accepting problems as opportunities for growth rather than obstacles, we can cultivate the resilience to overcome setbacks and come out stronger on the other side.

Investigating Root Causes: Determining the true causes of failures is essential to learning from them. We'll go over methods for carrying out in-depth investigations, pinpointing contributing elements, and obtaining a clear grasp of the dynamics underlying the setback.

Finding the Hidden Lessons for Personal Growth: There are lessons to be learned from setbacks in terms of personal growth. We will discuss how to take these lessons—be the about communication, decision-making, or personal habits—and use them as impetus for constructive change.

Developing a Growth mentality: When faced with obstacles, a growth mentality turns into a compass. By seeing obstacles as chances to grow and learn, we cultivate an attitude that is driven by constant improvement and transform failures into opportunities for both career and personal advancement.

Changing Approaches for Future Success:

Adapting approaches for future success is a necessary part of learning from mistakes. We'll talk about how learning from failures can help us make strategic changes that will make it easier for us to face future obstacles head-on and act more proactively.

Establishing Robust Coping Strategies:

Failures frequently put our coping strategies to the best. We'll look at how to build resilient coping mechanisms that support our mental health and enable us to handle adversity with poise and grace in addition to helping us weather setbacks.

The Function of Self-Awareness and Reflection:

Learning from failures can be facilitated by using reflection as a potent tool. We'll talk about how crucial self-awareness is to this process, stressing the need of reflection and comprehending how we react to failures in order to learn from them and move on.

Seeking Advice and Assistance: Asking for help while facing difficulties is a strength, not a weakness. We'll discuss the importance of peer support, counseling, and mentoring in the process of learning from failures, acknowledging that common experiences can offer insightful viewpoints.

Forgiveness and Moving Forward:
Forgiveness, both toward ourselves and others, is a practice that comes with learning from setbacks. We'll explore the transforming potential of letting go, which enables us to proceed with a refreshed sense of direction and wisdom.

Imagine every obstacle as a teacher, every misstep as a lesson, and every setback as a chance for significant personal development as we traverse the terrain of setbacks. With this investigation, may failures stop being roadblocks and turn into stepping stones leading to a resilient, enlightened, and ever-changing version of yourself.

7d: Seeking Support

Seeking Assistance: Handling Life's Obstacles Collectively

Support acts as a durable and interwoven thread in the complex tapestry that is our life. This investigation into getting help is a recognition of the power in compassionate relationships, life lessons learned from others, and the transformational effect of reaching out when faced with difficulties.

The Power of Vulnerability: Acknowledging one's own vulnerability as a source of strength is the first step in seeking support. We'll explore the transforming potential of being vulnerable with others, realizing that this creates connection and establishes the groundwork for genuine support.

Finding Supportive Networks: Finding and fostering supportive networks is a necessary step in creating a support system. In order to understand how each source of support adds to a varied and strong support network, we'll examine the many sources, including peer groups, mentors, professionals, and intimate friends and family.

Effective Communication:

Effective Communication is Key to Getting Help: Clearly stating our needs is a critical first step in getting assistance. We'll talk about how to communicate effectively, stressing the value of being clear in our expressions, establishing boundaries, and actively having candid conversations with people we can trust.

Counseling and Professional Support: When someone is in need, professional support is extremely important. We'll discuss the advantages of consulting with therapists, counselors, and other mental health specialists, appreciating their specific knowledge and skills in assisting with problem solving and promoting emotional health.

Peer Assistance and Mutual Experiences: This chapter provides valuable perspectives on the efficaciousness of peer support. Having experiences in common with those who have gone through comparable struggles fosters empathy, understanding, and comradery. We'll talk about how peer support is reciprocal and how it makes our journey richer.

Building Meaningful Relationships: Building meaningful relationships is a necessary step in asking for help. We'll discuss how forming close bonds with people fosters resilience, emotional support, and a sense of belonging while forming a network of relationships that helps us get through the highs and lows of life.

Active Listening and Empathy: These two qualities are necessary for being a supporting presence. We'll explore the skill of actually listening to people, demonstrating empathy, and creating a secure environment for communication. These abilities serve as the cornerstone of genuine and reciprocal assistance.

Overcoming Barriers and Stigma: This chapter discusses the stigma that is frequently attached to asking for help. We'll discuss strategies for overcoming both personal and cultural hurdles in order to promote an environment that welcomes candid discussions on emotional and mental health.

Promoting Empowerment and Self-Help: Seeking assistance entails more than just turning to other resources; it also entails empowering oneself.

We'll talk about self-help techniques, methods, and resources that people can use to improve their own mental health and feeling of agency.

The Ongoing Support Journey: As we grow, so does our need for support. We'll close by recognizing that getting help is a continuous process that changes as our lives do. We strengthen our interrelated human experience as a collective when we seek out and offer help.

May this exploration serve as a roadmap, a source of inspiration, and a gentle reminder that we are all connected by a common humanity that gives us the strength, resilience, and comfort to face life's obstacles together.

7e:Adaptability in Problem-Solving:

Handling Difficulties with Creative Remedies
This chapter examines the practice of flexible problem-solving, which is a strategy that, while dealing with life's complex issues, values creativity, adaptation, and a dynamic attitude. Come along on this exploration of flexible problem-solving and

learn how it enables people to deal with complexity with resiliency and creativity.

The Significance of Adaptability in Solving Problems:

Fundamentally, being flexible in problem-solving means being receptive to different approaches and having the capacity to modify plans of action in reaction to evolving conditions. We'll explore the code of this strategy and see how it develops a flexible and productive mindset while dealing with obstacles.

Accepting Creative Solutions: Being flexible encourages creativity when addressing issues. We'll examine the mutually beneficial link that exists between creativity and flexibility, realizing that thinking beyond the box frequently produces novel and unusual solutions.

Changing Strategies to the Situation: There is no one-size-fits-all approach to problem-solving. We'll talk about the significance of customizing tactics to the particular circumstances of every task, acknowledging that a flexible strategy entails evaluating and modifying techniques in light of the particulars of the current issue.

Resolving Issues through Iteration and Learning from Setbacks: Flexibility recognizes setbacks as essential to the resolution of issues. We'll look at how learning from mistakes and losses helps people grow personally and makes it possible to refine ideas over time for maximum impact.

Stabilizing Structure and Openness: Flexibility is the state of striking a balance between structure and openness; it does not entail chaos. We'll talk about how keeping an organized framework while being receptive to new ideas results in a flexible approach to problem-solving that changes with the circumstances.

Developing a Growth Mindset: Using a growth mindset as a foundational idea facilitates adaptable problem-solving. We'll explore how resilience and a positive approach to problem-solving are fostered by viewing problems as chances for learning and development.

Collaborative Problem-Solving and Effective Communication: This chapter provides insights into collaborative problem-solving. We'll examine how, by utilizing a variety of viewpoints and mutual insights, efficient communication within a team or with support networks improves the adaptability of problem-solving.

Leveraging Innovation and Technology: Adopting cutting-edge ideas and technology is another example of flexibility. We'll talk about how maintaining current with technology advancements and encouraging an inventive mentality support flexible problem-solving across a range of life areas.

Knowing When to Pivot: Being flexible requires the ability to recognize when to pivot. We'll look at how to spot clues that indicate a shift in course could be required so that people can adjust their plans and make well-informed judgments as situations change.

Developing Resilience Through Adaptable Solutions: This chapter's conclusion offers an analysis of how resilience is boosted by problem-solving adaptability. We'll talk about how having the flexibility to adjust and come up with solutions in a variety of circumstances fosters a resilient mentality that makes it easier to confidently take on new difficulties in the future.

Think of every obstacle you face on the path to flexible problem-solving as a chance to practice resilience, inventiveness, and adaptation. I hope this investigation sparks a creative approach to problem-solving that tackles current issues while also advancing an ongoing process of growth, learning, and invention.

7f: Developing a Compassionate Inner Dialogue through Positive Self-Talk

This chapter examines the practice of positive self-talk, which entails developing an encouraging and loving internal dialogue, and its capacity for transformation. Come along on this exploration of affirming self communication and see how it helps build resilience, positive thinking, and higher self-esteem.

Understanding Positive Self-Talk: We speak to ourselves using positive language, or positive self-talk. We'll explore the idea and learn how it affects our feelings, ideas, and way of thinking in general. Understanding the effects of our self-talk enables us to maximize its potential for personal development.

Cultivating Self-Compassion: Self-compassion is the foundation of constructive self-talk. We'll discuss how self-care for kindness, understanding, and patience is a necessary component of developing a compassionate inner dialogue. This routine turns into a pillar for enhancing mental health and resilience.

Taking On Negative Thought Patterns: A key component of positive self-talk is taking on negative thought patterns. We'll talk about techniques for recognizing and redefining self-limiting beliefs, enabling people to escape vicious cycles that erode self-worth and impede growth.

Affirmations for Empowerment: When used in constructive self-talk, affirmations may be very effective tools. We'll look at how deliberate use of empowering affirmations can build resilience, a good self-image, and a mindset that supports individual goals.

Developing a Growth Mindset: Developing a growth mindset is consistent with using positive self-talk. We'll explore how resilience, inventiveness, and self-belief in overcoming difficulties are enhanced when challenges are framed as opportunities for learning and growth.

Using Mindfulness in Self-Talk: This chapter provides guidance on how to use mindfulness in self-talk. We'll look at how being in the present moment enables people to watch their thoughts objectively and cultivates a calm and collected internal conversation.

Creating Optimistic Mental Images: Creating mental images that support an optimistic story is a component of positive self-talk. We'll talk about how visualization and uplifting thoughts support a more upbeat perspective, affecting feelings and behaviors that support individual objectives.

Stress-Reduction Techniques: Talking to oneself in a positive way helps reduce stress. We'll look at how practicing self-compassion, changing the way you think about stressful situations, and using affirmations to face obstacles head-on with a resilient and collected attitude can all help you manage stress.

Developing Self-Talk to Build Confidence: Self-talk that is constructive helps to build confidence. We'll talk about how recognizing accomplishments, concentrating on strengths, and use self-affirmations to boost self-esteem are all part of developing a confident inner dialogue.

Including good Self-Talk in Daily living: This chapter's conclusion offers helpful advice on how to include good self-talk into everyday living. We'll talk about how self-communication practices that are consistent and thoughtful can lead to long-lasting mental shifts that promote a more upbeat and resilient way of approaching life's obstacles.

Imagine positive self-talk as a kind and encouraging companion that will accompany you on your journey towards developing an optimistic, self-compassionate, and deeply held belief in your capacity to face life's challenges with grace and resiliency. This inner ally will support, encourage, and mentor you along the way.

7g: Maintaining a Growth Mindset

Sustaining a Growth Mindset: Fostering an Ongoing Process of Education and Improvement This chapter explores the idea of upholding a growth mindset, which is a positive outlook on life that welcomes difficulties, views setbacks as teaching moments, and cultivates the idea that one can always improve. Join us as we explore the ideas and methods that support a resilient and growing thinking.

Foundations of a Growth mentality: The idea that intelligence and skill may be acquired over time is important to the maintenance of a growth mentality. We'll explore the fundamental ideas and comprehend how this way of thinking influences perspectives on effort, learning, and conquering challenges.

Accepting Difficulties as Chances:
Keeping a growth mindset entails viewing obstacles as opportunities to improve. We'll look at how people who have a growth mindset see challenges as chances for learning and growth rather than as obstacles to overcome.

Learning from Failures and Setbacks: When one adopts a growth attitude, failures and setbacks serve as priceless teachers. We'll talk about the transforming potential of viewing setbacks as a necessary component of learning, which enables people to draw conclusions, refine approaches, and persevere in the face of difficulty.

The Path to Mastery: A growth mindset sees effort as an essential element of success. We'll explore the idea that mastery and reaching one's greatest potential can only be attained through consistent work and a passion for learning.

Building a Good Relationship with Criticism:
When one adopts a development attitude, criticism serves as a tool for improvement rather than as a discouragement. We'll look at how people who have this perspective see constructive criticism as

important information for growth, encouraging a healthy relationship with criticism and ongoing introspection.

Fostering a passion of Learning: Beyond the confines of formal schooling, a growth mindset fosters a passion of learning. We'll talk about how pursuing new knowledge and skills with a curiosity-driven mindset leads to a happy and meaningful existence.

Sustaining a growth mentality requires modeling perseverance for both oneself and other people in the face of setbacks. We'll look at how exhibiting tenacity in the face of adversity creates the foundation for a resilient mindset and encourages others to take on problems with hope and tenacity.

As the chapter progresses, it becomes clear how important it is to foster a collaborative and supportive workplace. We'll talk about how creating a cooperative and encouraging environment supports and maintains a growth mentality in people as well as communities, whether in interpersonal or professional contexts.

Managing Short-Term and Long-Term Objectives: People with a growth mindset strike a balance between their immediate objectives and their long-term vision. We'll explore the tactical method of establishing attainable benchmarks while maintaining focus on broad goals, establishing a structure for ongoing growth and accomplishment.

Milestones and Achievements: Keeping a growth mentality calls for acknowledging and appreciating all accomplishments, no matter how modest. We'll talk about how celebrating successes and turning points strengthens self-belief in one's ability to progress and inspires further study and advancement.

Think of the terrain of sustaining a development mindset as a dynamic journey, one that requires constant learning, adaptation, and evolution. I hope this exploration encourages you to rise to challenges, see opportunities in setbacks, and develop a mindset that will lead you to a lifetime of constant progress and fulfillment.

7h: Building Coping Strategies Developing Coping Techniques: Strengthening Your Toolkit for Resilience

This chapter delves into the process of creating coping strategies, which are customized tools meant to help people face life's obstacles head-on and with grace. Join us as we explore the ideas and methods that enable people to lay a solid foundation for their emotional health and efficient stress management.

Comprehending Coping Strategies: Coping strategies refer to the methods and instruments people employ to handle stress, overcome obstacles, and preserve their mental health. We'll explore the idea, realizing that developing resilience requires a wide range of coping mechanisms.

Identifying Personal Stressors: A thorough awareness of one's own stressors is the cornerstone of good coping. We'll look at techniques for pinpointing particular stresses and triggers, enabling people to customize their coping mechanisms to meet their own set of problems.

Creating Adaptive Coping Mechanisms: Adaptive coping means finding healthy and constructive ways to deal with stress. We'll talk about how adaptive coping methods evolve, emphasizing the value of tactics that support long-term emotional health as opposed to offering momentary solace.

Developing a Holistic Approach: Coping mechanisms work best when they cover a range of life experiences. We'll discuss the value of using a comprehensive strategy that takes into account social, emotional, and physical aspects of wellbeing in order to create a complete toolset for coping.

Relaxation Techniques and Mindfulness: Developing mindfulness becomes essential for managing stress. We'll explore mindfulness and relaxation techniques, emphasizing methods that promote inner peace, reduce stress, and foster a present-centered awareness.

Efficient Time Management: Efficient time management is a useful coping technique. We'll talk about how time management, prioritization, and organizational abilities help people feel less stressed and more in charge of their daily lives.

Social Support Systems: Coping is frequently a team effort. We'll discuss the value of social support systems and how relationships may offer emotional support, comprehension, and a feeling of community when things are hard.

Positive Thinking and Cognitive Restructuring: Reframing unfavorable thought patterns is a key component of cognitive restructuring. We'll talk about how resilience is cultivated by adopting an optimistic outlook and confronting self-limiting beliefs, which in turn fosters an emotional wellbeing-promoting mentality.

Physical activity and wellness practices: Emotional toughness and physical wellness are linked. We'll discuss how wellness routines and physical activity can be incorporated into coping mechanisms, acknowledging the dual advantages of engaging in activities that support mental and physical well-being.

Creative outlets and Self-expression:

Expressing oneself creatively serves as a stress-relieving and self-expression mechanism. We'll talk about how coping mechanisms might include creative expression and emotional release through the use of arts, writing, or music.

Getting Professional Help When Needed: One

of the most important coping skills is knowing when to get professional help. We'll talk about how people can identify when they need more help with their coping mechanisms and how getting help from mental health or counseling specialists helps people cope more effectively.

Frequent Reflection and Adjustment: A

summary of the significance of regular reflection and adjustment is provided in the chapter's conclusion. We'll talk about how coping mechanisms are dynamic and may require regular evaluation and adjustment to accommodate changing conditions and personal development.

When you start the process of developing coping mechanisms, see it as a never-ending investigation—a constant process of finding, honing, and incorporating resources that strengthen your resilience and enable you to face life's obstacles head-on with courage and flexibility.

7i: Emotional Regulation Techniques:

Emotional Control Methods: Promoting Equilibrium in the Internal Environment
The art of emotional regulation—a competent practice that entails comprehending, regulating, and navigating one's emotions in a way that promotes inner balance and wellbeing—is examined in this chapter. Come explore a range of methods that enable people to develop emotional fortitude and reserve balance in the always shifting field of emotions.

Comprehending Emotional Regulation: The capacity to control and adjust one's emotional reactions is known as emotional regulation. We'll explore the idea and acknowledge that this ability is fundamental to preserving mental well-being, cultivating wholesome relationships, and gracefully overcoming obstacles in life.

Emotional management and Mindfulness Meditation: Mindfulness meditation is a fundamental component of emotional management. We'll look at techniques that develop present-moment awareness, which enables people to notice their feelings without passing judgment and promotes composed, composed responses.

Exercises for Deep Breathing that Calm the Nervous System: Deep breathing exercises provide a direct route to calm the nervous system. We'll talk about methods like box breathing and diaphragmatic breathing and examine how deliberate breathwork encourages emotional balance and relaxation.

How to Ground Yourself and Remain Present: Practicing grounding keeps people rooted in the here and now. We'll look at techniques that help people stay grounded and centered during periods of high emotional intensity, include sensory grounding, establishing a connection with the surroundings, and grounding affirmations.

Journaling as a Tool for Emotional Expression: Journaling is a tool for introspection and emotional expression. We'll talk about how writing about feelings, experiences, and ideas offers a healthy outlet and helps with emotional regulation by fostering self-awareness and comprehension.

Examining and rephrasing unfavorable thinking patterns is a key component of cognitive restructuring for thought awareness. We'll look at methods for reframing and challenging negative ideas in order to cultivate a more optimistic and well-rounded outlook when dealing with difficult emotions.

Progressive Muscle Relaxation for Physical Release: Strong emotions are frequently accompanied by physical tightness. We'll talk about progressive muscle relaxation, a method that helps people relax physically and reduce emotional tension by gradually testing and relaxing different muscle groups.

Expressive Arts Therapy for Creativity and Release: Creating art through expressive mediums like music, painting, or sketching provides a creative outlet for expressing emotions. We'll look at how various artistic mediums can be used as therapeutic tools to help people understand and let go of their feelings.

Self-Compassion Techniques for Calming: Self-compassion techniques can ease emotional pain. We'll talk about methods for creating a loving and supportive inner relationship with oneself by treating oneself with compassion, empathy, and self-soothing actions.

Exercise and Mindful Movements for Energy Release: Engaging in physical activity opens up a pathway for the release of emotional energy. We'll look at mindful movement techniques and workout regimens that encourage the release of stored-up energy and support a feeling of balance and vigor.

Social Connection as Emotional Support: Having relationships with other people is a great way to manage your emotions. We will go over the significance of preserving social connections, getting help, and communicating feelings to people you can trust as part of an all-encompassing approach to emotional wellness.

Using Mindful Eating to Increase Sensory Awareness: During meals, mindful eating techniques increase awareness of your senses. We'll look at how focusing on the tastes, textures, and feelings of food can help with emotional regulation by offering a peaceful and grounding experience.

As you investigate these methods for regulating emotions, picture them as a variety of instruments in your inner toolbox, each with a specific function in promoting resilience, self-awareness, and emotional equilibrium. I hope your journey toward emotional regulation is a kind investigation of the complex terrain that is your inner life.

7j:Self-Compassion Practices

Exercises for Self-Compassion: Developing the Gentle Art of Self-Care

The transforming potential of self-compassion practices—a kind and compassionate method of self-care that promotes resilience, emotional health, and a gentler relationship with oneself—is examined in this chapter. Join us as we explore a range of methods that enable people to develop self-compassion and treat themselves with the same kindness and understanding that they show to others.

Comprehending Self-Compassion:

Self-compassion refers to the act of showing love, understanding, and acceptance to oneself, particularly in times of hardship or adversity. We will explore the idea, realizing that emotional resilience and general welfare are based on self-compassion.

The primary practice of mindfulness is the practice of mindful self-compassion meditation. We'll look at guided meditations that help develop a compassionate awareness of one's own suffering and offer consoling and reassuring messages to oneself, creating an atmosphere of inner warmth and nurturing.

Composing Letters of Self-Compassion:

Composing letters of self-compassion is a therapeutic activity. We'll talk about the habit of writing oneself a letter of love and understanding, acknowledging difficulties, expressing support, and providing words of wisdom when things are tough.

Body Scan for Self-Acceptance: The body scan can be used as a tool for self-acceptance if it is conducted through a self-compassionate lens. We'll look at how developing a non-judgmental awareness and scanning the body attentively can help one feel compassionate toward oneself and appreciate one's body.

Self-Compassionate Affirmations: A self-compassionate tone permeates affirmations. We'll speak about crafting and repeating affirmations that highlight compassion, acceptance of oneself, and positive self-talk in order to create a caring internal dialogue.

Grounded Presence with Mindful Walking: Self-compassion combined with mindful walking transforms it into a grounded presence practice. We'll look at how walking deliberately, focusing on each step and the scenery, can be a kind of moving meditation that cultivates self-compassion.

Gratitude Journaling as a Tool for Self-Appreciation: Keeping a gratitude notebook can help you learn to appreciate yourself. We'll talk about the process of identifying and documenting instances of self-love, maintaining an optimistic mindset, and developing thankfulness for one's own advantages.

Self-Compassionate Visualization: Self-compassion is the main emphasis of visualization techniques. We'll talk about guided visualizations, which entail imagining oneself in a supportive, understanding, and warm environment that promotes self-compassion and a sense of security.

Calm Self-Touch Techniques: Calm self-touch techniques turn into self-care gestures. We'll talk about methods like putting a hand on the heart or giving yourself a consoling embrace, investigating how these corporal acts might arise feelings of warmth and compassion for oneself.

Self-compassion and mindful breathing techniques go hand in hand when it comes to emotional management. We'll study self-kindness-focus breathing practices that use the breath as a grounding anchor when experiencing emotional upheaval.

Self-Compassion Breaks in Daily living:

Taking compassionate breaks is a key component of incorporating self-compassion into daily living. We'll talk about quick activities, or "self-compassion breaks," that people may add into their daily routines to provide self-kindness and relaxation in the midst of life's hectic schedules.

Reflective Self-Inquiry as a Tool for Understanding: Compassionate

self-understanding can be achieved through reflective self-inquiry. We'll look at questions and prompts that promote introspection and provide a kind and sympathetic perspective on one's needs, difficulties, and goals.

Imagine these self-compassion exercises as gentle and loving acts that you are doing for yourself. They are an invitation to be open, kind, and compassionate to yourself, to celebrate your strengths, to embrace your vulnerabilities, and to ride the ups and downs of life with a heart that is open, kind, and compassionate toward the beautiful journey that is uniquely yours.

Chapter 8:Embracing Change Navigating Life Transitions with Confidence

On life's path, change is an inevitable companion that brings with it new experiences, opportunities, and problems. Accepting change is an art, one that gives people the ability to move through changes with fortitude, self-assurance, and a sense of direction. This chapter will examine how negotiating life changes may be transformative, recognizing the uncertainty that change brings and identifying the inner qualities that emerge when faced with change.

8a..Determining Your Own Values:

Seeing Your Life's guiding stars
This chapter sets out on a contemplative journey to discover and analyze personal values—a compass that directs choices, establishes priorities, and gives life depth and significance. Join us as we explore the fundamental ideas and concepts that underpin your identity, guiding you in making decisions and directing your behavior toward what really matters.

Realizing the Importance of Personal : A person's personal values are the core ideals and convictions that are extremely important to them. We will explore the idea that living a life that is consistent with these principles provides meaning, clarity, and an authentic experience.

Thinking Deeply About Basic Beliefs:
Determining one's own values necessitates thinking deeply about one's basic beliefs. We'll talk about methods and exercises that promote reflection, enabling people to delve into the ideas that really speak to them and shapes who they are.

Examining Values in Various Life Domains:
Values show up in a variety of life domains, including relationships, work, personal development, and more. We'll look at how one's personal values might vary in different contexts and how identifying these differences can help one understand their guiding principles more fully.

Finding Your Values from Life events: Life events provide important windows into one's own values. We'll talk about how important life experiences and turning points can help people find and define their beliefs, open doors to self-discovery, and gain a better knowledge of what really matters.

Aligning Values with Life Objectives: Using values as a guide, one can set and accomplish worthwhile objectives. We'll look at how a strong synergy is produced when personal values and life objectives are in line, inspiring people to seek goals that are consistent with their fundamental beliefs.

Setting Personal Values as a Priority in Decision-Making: Making decisions is improved by knowing one's own values. We'll talk about methods for giving values top priority when faced with options so that people can choose what's right for them and lead fulfilling lives.

Making a Values-founded Action Plan: An action plan that is founded on values converts ideas into concrete steps. We'll look at how people might make a plan that synchronizes their everyday activities with their values, helping them live more purposefully and morally every day.

Handling Difficulties with Values: When faced with difficulties, values serve as a beacon of guidance. We will talk about how a person can overcome hardship with grace and purpose by drawing strength, resilience, and direction from their personal beliefs when things are tough.

Communicating Values in Relationships: Relationship dynamics are shaped by values. We'll look at how sharing personal beliefs effectively promote comprehension and a sense of connection in interpersonal and professional relationships, which in turn leads to mutual respect and a sense of shared purpose.

Values Changing Over Time: Individual values are dynamic and subject to change. We'll talk about how values naturally evolve over the course of a person's life, taking into account the fact that growth and self-discovery can cause changes in what is significant at different times.

Cultivating Consistency with ideals: Consistency is necessary to live in accordance with one's particular ideals. We'll look at how developing routines and conduct that align with one's principles leads to congruence, which in turn promotes authenticity and a closer relationship with oneself.

Thinking Back on Values as a Source of Appreciation and thankfulness: Values provide a basis for appreciation and thankfulness. We'll talk about the significance of taking time to consider and be grateful for the tenets that give life meaning and enhance one's sense of fulfillment and contentment.

When you set out to discover your personal values, see the process as an investigation of the distinct constellation that forms your life. I hope that this journey will shine light on the guiding stars that will direct you toward a life that is true, meaningful, and deeply connected to what really matters.

8b: Goal Setting in Transition

Establishing Objectives in Transition:
Choosing a Meaningful Path During Shift
This chapter covers goal-setting in the context of life transitions—a dynamic process that enables people to steer a meaningful route through change. Come learn how to create objectives that mean something, use changes as a chance to grow, and create a feeling of purpose and fulfillment for the journey ahead.

Realizing the Power of Goal Setting in Transition: When a person is going through a change in life, goal setting may be a very useful tool. We'll explore the idea that establishing specific, meaningful goals gives one a feeling of purpose, direction, and a road map for navigating the constantly shifting terrain of change.

Accepting Change as a Spark for Objective Investigation:

Goal exploration presents a special opportunity during transitions. We'll talk about how life transitions provide people with opportunities to re-evaluate their priorities, aspirations, and future prospects, leading them to create objectives that are in line with their changing circumstances and ideals.

Goal Alignment with Personal Values during Transitions: Goals must be realigned with personal values during transitions. We'll look at how to make sure that objectives stay true to one's guiding values and help people feel authentic and purposeful throughout times of transition.

Establishing SMART Objectives: SMART objectives offer a structured framework for achievement because they are Specific, Measurable, Achievable, Relevant, and Time-Bound. We'll talk about how using the SMART criteria improves goal setting's efficacy by generating specific, doable targets that help people move closer to their intended results.

Setting Both Short-Term and Long-Term Objectives: Transitions frequently require a combination of short-term fixes and long-term ambitions. We'll discuss how creating a balance between short- and long-term goals helps people meet short-term demands without losing sight of long-term ambitions.

Promoting Adaptability in Goal-Setting:
During times of transition, goal-setting requires flexibility. We'll talk about how important it is to promote flexibility, acknowledging that the dynamic nature of change may call for modifications to objectives and plans in order to assure advancement in the face of unforeseen difficulties.

Dividing Bigger Objectives Into Doable Steps:
Dividing big objectives into doable steps makes them more attainable. We'll look at techniques for breaking down big goals into smaller, manageable tasks, encouraging a sense of accomplishment, and sustaining motivation during the changeover.

Including Learning and Growth Objectives:
Changes offer chances for education and development of the self. We'll talk about how learning and growth objectives can be incorporated into the goal-setting process to help people take

advantage of the transformative potential that comes with times of transition.

Juggling Personal and Professional Objectives

Changes in life frequently have an effect on both the personal and professional spheres. We'll discuss how to strike a balance between your personal and professional goals, encouraging a comprehensive goal-setting strategy that takes into account all facets of your life.

Seeking Assistance in Pursuing Your Goals:

Having a support network enhances your goal pursuit. We'll talk about how crucial it is to build a network of people who can offer accountability, support, and encouragement during times of transition, whether it comes from friends, family, mentors, or professional networks.

Celebrating Achievements and Milestones:

Setting goals requires acknowledging progress along the way. We'll discuss the value of acknowledging and appreciating accomplishments, no matter how big or small, as they provide a sense of fulfillment and inspiration to help people move forward with their shift.

Goal-Setting Reflection and Adjustment:
Regular goal-setting increases the efficacy of the process. We'll talk about the need of reviewing progress, reevaluating objectives, and adjusting as necessary to keep goals in line with changing circumstances and desires.

Cultivating Resilience in the Pursuit of Goals:
Resilience is a helpful ally in the pursuit of goals during changes. We'll look at how developing resilience—accepting failures as a necessary part of the process—nurtures the tenacity required to face obstacles and remain dedicated to one's objectives.

When you create goals for yourself amid life transitions, see it as an active process of empowerment and self-awareness. May your objectives act as beacons of light, showing the way ahead in the face of change and encouraging a feeling of direction, fulfillment, and personal development as you embark on your life-changing adventure.

8c:Establishing a Support Network

Creating a Support System: Creating Strong Foundations During Transitions

This chapter explores the crucial topic of creating a support system, which is a basic framework that offers bravery, understanding, and support throughout periods of transition. Join this investigation into the art of developing relationships, making meaningful connections, and building a network of support that can withstand life's ups and downs.

Understanding the Value of a Support System: During times of change, emotional health is greatly aided by having a strong support system. We'll explore the idea that forming relationships with others provides a safety net during times of transition by providing shared understanding, emotional support, and a sense of belonging.

Finding Important People in Your Network: Diverse people are frequently a part of successful support networks. We'll talk about how to find important individuals—friends, relatives, mentors, coworkers, our experts—who can offer distinctive viewpoints, direction, and support to various facets of your life.

Building Real ties: The foundation of a support system is made up of genuine ties. We'll talk about how important it is to build sincere, reciprocal relationships in which people can assist one another in a spirit of trust and understanding and share their strengths and vulnerabilities.

Diversifying Your Support System: A network of supporters is made stronger by diversity. We'll talk about the advantages of having a wide variety of people in your network, each bringing unique perspectives, abilities, and ways to help, building a strong and durable support system.

Effectively Communicating Your Needs: In a support network, open communication is crucial. We'll talk about how to build understanding and a supportive atmosphere with people in your support system by successfully articulating your requirements, preferences, and boundaries.

Developing Emotional Resilience Through Relationships: Emotional resilience is influenced by support systems. We'll talk about how social ties give you emotional support, motivation, and a feeling of humanity that makes it easier to overcome obstacles and overcome misfortune.

Seeking Expert Assistance When Required:
An important part of a support network is expert assistance. We'll discuss how adding a layer of knowledge to your support network by getting advice from counselors, therapists, or other mental health professionals is crucial when dealing with difficult situations.

Maintaining a Balance in ties: In a support system, ties are strengthened through reciprocity. We'll talk about the significance of striking a balance between giving and receiving, acknowledging that reciprocal assistance creates a sense of shared accountability and fortifies the times within your network.

Handling Relationship Changes: Relationships may be impacted by life transitions. We'll talk about how to handle relationship transitions so that your network of support can change with you while still being a trustworthy and connected source.

Engaging in Community Support:

Communities offer a collective strength. We'll talk about the advantages of becoming a part of online or offline support groups where people going through similar struggles can exchange advice, encouragement, and experiences.

Setting Up Boundaries for Self-Care: In a

support system, sound boundaries are essential. We'll talk about how setting boundaries may safeguard your wellbeing and make sure the people in your network are beneficial to your development and fortitude.

Gratitude-Sharing Within Your Network:

Gratitude fosters relationships. We'll talk about how important it is to show your thanks to the people in your support system and recognize how their presence, encouragement, and support have impacted your path.

Periodic Assessment and Modification:

Assistance networks undergo changes. We'll talk about the significance of routine review and modification, acknowledging that your support system could require a review as your situation changes to make sure it still meets your changing needs.

Building an Empathy and Understanding Culture: A support system is held together by empathy. We'll talk about building a compassionate and understanding culture in your network—a place where people may feel accepted, understood, and supported without passing judgment.

Imagine your support network as a dynamic web of links that offers resilience and strength as you begin the process of building one. May your network of support grow to be a wellspring of consolation, inspiration, and wisdom, providing a strong base as you manage life's ups and downs.

8d: Embracing Uncertainty

Accepting Uncertainty: Bravery and Resilience in the Face of the Unknown
This chapter delves into the life-changing process of accepting uncertainty—a capability that enables

people to face the unknown with bravery, flexibility, and fortitude. Come along for this journey into the practice of developing a positive outlook, accepting life's inherent volatility, and finding comfort in ambiguity.

Recognizing the Nature of Uncertainty: Being uncertain is a natural aspect of being human. We'll explore the idea that uncertainty is a fundamental part of existence and that it shapes both our individual and societal narratives.

Changing Attitudes Toward Possibility: Adapting to uncertainty necessitates a mental change. We'll look at ways to reframe uncertainty as a space of opportunity where fresh development, chances, and discoveries might materialize, leading to an optimistic and receptive mindset.

Developing Adaptability in the Face of Change: Handling uncertainty requires the ability to adapt. We'll talk about how developing adaptability—being willing to alter and adjust to new situations—improves resilience and gives people the ability to prosper in unpredictable times.

Accommodating Ambiguity: Accommodating ambiguity is a talent that must be taught. We'll look at methods for finding comfort when things are unclear, enabling people to welcome ambiguity as a place where ideas can flow and new stories can be revealed.

Present-Moment Mindfulness: In uncertain times, mindfulness serves as a beacon of guidance. We'll talk about practicing mindful presence, which lowers anxiety about the uncertain future by concentrating on the present as a source of stability and clarity.

Accepting Change as a Constant: Uncertainty frequently coexists with change, which is a constant. We'll look at how accepting change as a normal and constant part of life builds resilience and makes it easier for people to go through changes.

Developing Resilience Through Uncertainty: Resilience can be developed in an uncertain platform. We'll talk about how confronting difficulties and unknowns helps people become more resilient, which helps them overcome hardships and failures.

Examining the Power of Flexibility: In unpredictable times, flexibility can be a valuable asset. We'll look at the value of flexibility in adjusting to shifting conditions, shifting perspectives, and enjoying life's flux.

Learning from Uncertain Events: Uncertain events can impart important knowledge. We'll talk about how important it is to think back on and draw lessons from uncertain times in order to gain personal development and a better understanding of oneself.

Juggling Acceptance and Planning: While acceptance is important, planning is also necessary. We'll go into the skill of striking a balance between acceptance and strategic planning, understanding that although plans and objectives offer guidance, it's also sage to let the path take its natural course.

Encouraging Curiosity: In confusing situations, curiosity serves as a compass. We'll talk about how curiosity helps people face the unknown with an open mind and see uncertainty as a chance for exploration and learning.

Developing Self-Compassion in Uncertain Times: When faced with uncertainty, self-compassion is a comforting salve. We'll look at exercises that promote self-compassion, which enables people to be kind and sympathetic to themselves when they're feeling uncertain or confused.

Getting in Touch with Support Systems: Support networks are essential for negotiating uncertainty. We'll talk about the value of forming relationships with mentors, friends, and family in order to build a network that provides support, direction, and a common sense of resilience.

Accepting Uncertainty as a Growth-Catalyst: Uncertainty promotes both spiritual and personal development. We'll look at how having a growth-oriented attitude and accepting uncertainty can result in significant learning, self-discovery, and potential development.

I hope that learning to embrace uncertainty will help you on your journey by giving you the confidence, resiliency, and curiosity to turn doubt into a blank canvas full of endless possibilities.

8e: Developing Adaptability

Increasing Adaptability: Handling Change with Agility and Resilience
This chapter delves into the critical talent of cultivating adaptation, which equips people to deal with change with fortitude, dexterity, and optimism. Come learn how to be flexible, learn from changes, and develop the ability to adapt so that you can succeed in life's ever-changing terrain.

Acknowledging the Value of Adaptability:
Being adaptable is essential when dealing with change. We'll explore the idea that developing adaptability involves more than just knowing how to react in certain circumstances; rather, it involves developing a core competency that improves one's general capacity to deal with life's unforeseen turns.

Accepting the Dynamics of Change:
Adaptability necessitates accepting the dynamic nature of change, which is a constant. We'll talk

about the mental shift that's required to see change as a natural and frequently advantageous part of life, which lays the groundwork for adaptability.

Developing a Growth-Oriented Mentality:
Adaptability is fueled by a growth-oriented mentality. We'll look at techniques for developing a mindset that sees obstacles as chances for development and learning, leading to a positive outlook on change.

Learning from Changes and Difficulties:
Changes and difficulties present important opportunities for learning. We will talk about the value of actively learning from experiences—both good and bad—in order to develop flexibility and acquire knowledge that will help one become more resilient in the future.

Developing Thinking Flexibility: Developing thinking flexibility is essential to being adaptable. We'll look at ways to improve cognitive flexibility, or the capacity to be receptive to many viewpoints and methods and hence improve one's capacity to deal with a variety of circumstances.

Developing Mindful Awareness: Being mindfully aware improves flexibility. We will talk about the importance of mindfulness in maintaining awareness of the present moment, staying in the present, and encouraging an adaptive response by avoiding unwarranted resistance to change.

Developing Emotional Resilience: The foundation of flexibility is emotional resilience. We'll look at techniques for developing emotional resilience, which enables people to deal with the difficult emotions that come with transition in a balanced, self-aware, and resilient manner.

Looking for Learning Opportunities: Ongoing education is essential for adaptability. We'll talk about how being flexible in a world that is constantly changing requires actively seeking out learning opportunities, whether through formal education, skill development, or experience learning.

Managing Uncertainty with Confidence: Adaptability helps one feel confident when things are unclear. We'll look at how people who have a high capacity for adaptation may more confidently manage difficult situations and see the unknown as a place to explore and grow.

Promoting Open Communication:

Relationships and organizations that are flexible benefit from open communication. We'll talk about the value of encouraging open, honest communication as a means of promoting the sharing of concepts, criticism, and flexible solutions.

Promoting Collaborative Problem-Solving:

Cooperation makes people more adaptive. We'll discuss the advantages of collaborative problem-solving, in which many viewpoints are combined to handle issues and produce original ideas that enhance overall flexibility.

Embracing Change and Adapting to It: The first step towards adaptation is acceptance. We'll talk about how important it is to accept and acknowledge changes so that people can get over resistance and proactively adjust to their new environment.

Honoring Adaptive Accomplishments: Giving credit for adaptable accomplishments encourages drive. We'll discuss the significance of acknowledging instances in which flexibility had favorable results, highlighting the relevance of this capacity and inspiring further development.

Maintaining a Balance between Structure and Flexibility: Structure offers stability, while flexibility permits adaptation. We'll talk about how to strike a healthy balance between the requirement for flexibility and structure, adapting to the demands of various circumstances.

Developing a Sense of Humor: Laughter makes change easier to bear. We'll discuss how humor helps people become more adaptive by giving them a humorous viewpoint that reduce stress and encourages perseverance in the face of adversity.

I hope that learning about becoming more adaptable can help you along the way by giving you the tools you need to handle change with fortitude, dexterity, and a mindset that views setbacks as chances for improvement.

8f:Self-Reflection in Change

Self-Reflection in Transition: Fostering Development by Self-Examination

This chapter examines the practice of self-reflection, which may be a powerful tool for fostering insight, resilience in the face of change, and personal growth. Come learn about the practice of introspection, developing self-awareness, and using reflective inquiry as a guide to help you through the challenges of life's changes.

Acknowledging Self-Reflection's Power:

Self-reflection is a powerful tool for personal development. We'll explore the idea that setting aside time for introspection enables people to better comprehend their own ideas, feelings, and actions, leading to a stronger sense of self-awareness.

Making Room for Reflection: Contemplation necessitates deliberate space. We'll talk about how to carve out time in the busyness of life for moments of quiet introspection and silence so that people may connect with their inner selves and find clarity in the face of change.

Developing an Inquisitive and Open Mind: Effective self-reflection requires an inquisitive and open mind. We'll talk about how critical it is to approach self-reflection with curiosity and welcome the chance to examine one's ideas and feelings without passing judgment.

Establishing Intentional Goals for Self-Reflection: Goals give self-reflection direction. We'll look at the technique of establishing deliberate goals for self-reflection, which help to direct the process and lead to more meaningful and targeted introspection. These goals can be certain regions or facts of life to examine.

Journaling as a Reflective Tool: Keeping a journal helps one reflect on oneself. We'll talk about the advantages of maintaining a reflective diary, which gives people a physical place to express their feelings, ideas, and observations and promotes a better understanding of themselves.

Examining basic Beliefs and Values: A key component of self-reflection is the examination of basic beliefs and values. We'll explore the process of identifying and analyzing guiding principles, acknowledging the ways in which these values influence judgments, choices, and reactions to change.

Analyzing Thought and Behavior Patterns: Patterns provide self-reflection. We'll look at the technique of analyzing recurrent thought and behavior patterns to identify routines that help or impede personal development while things are changing.

Identifying Emotional Reactions to Change: When engaging in introspection, emotions can offer important insights. We'll talk about how crucial it is to identify and comprehend people's emotional reactions to change so they can traverse the nuances of their emotions and utilize them as cues to reflect.

Evaluating Oneself: Self-reflection provides an opportunity to evaluate one's strengths and places for improvement. We'll look at methods for assessing one's own abilities objectively, acknowledging accomplishments, and pinpointing areas that could use more work.

Linking Historical Experiences to Current Change: Historical experiences influence how we react to change now. We'll talk about how making the connection between previous experiences and present changes helps people see trends, learn from them, and use their past skills to their advantage when facing new obstacles.

Developing Mindful Awareness: Reflecting on oneself is improved by mindful awareness. We'll look at techniques for developing awareness, staying in the present, and creating a heightened consciousness that enhances the quality of introspection.

Establishing Self-Compassionate Intentions: Self-compassion serves as a foundational idea in introspection. We'll talk about how important it is to make self-compassionate intentions, accept that growth and self-discovery entail challenges, and treat oneself with love.

Asking for Feedback to Gain Personal Understanding: Feedback offers outside viewpoints. We'll discuss the benefits of getting

input from mentors, coworkers, or close friends in
order to develop a more complete self-image and
acquire new perspectives.

Organizing Reaction-Based Action Steps:
Action is informed by reflection. We'll talk about the
process of turning self-reflective insights into doable
actions, laying up a plan for one's own development
and deliberate reactions to change.

Making Self-Reflection a Constant Practice:
Self-reflection requires consistency. We'll discuss
how to include self-reflection into everyday
activities and make it a habit to promote constant
personal development and flexibility.

I hope that the process of self-reflection will
energize and enlighten you, enabling you to navigate
life's always shifting terrain with fortitude, wisdom,
and a profound comprehension of your changing
identity.

8g: Making Conscious Decisions:

Making Decisions with Presence and Clarity

This chapter delves into the practice of mindful decision-making, which is a transforming strategy that helps people make decisions with clarity, presence, and a keen understanding of their intents and beliefs. Come learn about the concepts of mindfulness, how to maintain composure when making decisions, and how to choose decisions that are true to who you are.

Grasping the Concept of Mindful Decision-Making: Conscious and present awareness are key components of mindful decision-making. We'll explore the idea that making decisions while paying attention improves decision-making clarity, lower stress levels, and encourages decisions that are consistent with one's values.

Developing an award Presence: Making decisions is predicated on having an award presence. We'll look at techniques for developing present awareness, enabling people to fully participate in the decision-making process, and encouraging a focused, clear head.

Accepting Non-Judgmental Observation: A crucial component of mindfulness is non-judgmental observation. We'll talk about how to observe ideas, feelings, and outside circumstances without passing judgment right away in order to provide room for objective awareness when making decisions.

Making fundamental Values and Intentions Clear: Well-considered choices are consistent with fundamental values. We'll talk about how important it is to make decisions that are in line with one's true self by making clear one's aims and own ideals.

Building Emotional Intelligence: Making better decisions is facilitated by emotional intelligence. We'll talk about how emotional awareness and regulation help people make decisions by enabling them to move intelligently and in balance through the emotional terrain.

Putting Grounding strategies into Practice: Grounding strategies offer solidity in the face of decisions. We'll look at mindfulness-based grounding techniques to help you make decisions with stability and serenity, like deep breathing and anchoring in the here and now.

Reflection and Action must be Balanced:
Making thoughtful decision requires striking a balance between the two. We'll talk about how to strike a balance between carefully weighing your alternatives and acting decisively, making sure that decisions are made promptly and with sufficient knowledge.

Developing an Open Mind: Having an open mind makes decision-making more flexible. We'll look at methods for fostering open-mindedness, which enables people to take into account a range of viewpoints and options and makes decisions that are more flexible and creative.

Acknowledging Prejudices in Decision-Making: Making thoughtful decision requires awareness of prejudgment. We'll talk about typical decision-making biases and strategies for identifying and lessening their impact in order to encourage more deliberate and objective choices.

Putting Non-Attachment to Outcomes into Practice

Practice: Making decisions with non-attachment promotes resilience. We'll talk about the idea of practicing non-attachment to particular results, letting people make choices without feeling bound by certain expectations, and accepting that outcomes are always changing.

Reflective Inquiry: Reflective inquiry enhances comprehension. We'll discuss how to encourage people to consider their motives, possible outcomes, and how their decisions connect with their values by encouraging them to ask thoughtful questions during the decision-making process.

Including Conscious Decision-Making in Everyday Life:

Making thoughtful decisions is a way of life. We'll talk about incorporating mindfulness into everyday decisions, acknowledging that the concepts of awareness and present can improve choices that range from the trivial to the important.

Managing Making Decisions in the Face of Uncertainty:

A thoughtful decision-making process thrives on ambiguity. We'll talk about how to make decisions in the face of uncertainty by applying mindfulness to gain perspective and come to decisions that feel real and rooted.

Using Mindfulness in Group Decision-Making: Group situations are one area where mindfulness is applicable. We'll talk about how people can practice mindfulness in group decision-making, creating a setting where values and awareness are shared and influence group decisions.

Taking Lessons from Decision Outcomes: Decision outcomes offer possibilities for learning. We'll look at the process of accepting failures and achievements as important teaching moments that support continuous development on the personal and professional fronts.

I hope that practicing mindful decision-making will empower you and lead you to make decisions that are true to who you are and that will help you navigate the difficult decisions that lie ahead.

8h: Seeking Expert Advice: Handling Difficulties with Professional Assistance

This chapter delves into the process of seeking professional counsel, which can be a transforming tool for people who are facing doubts or obstacles or who want to improve personally. Come explore the advantages of seeking advice from specialists, identifying suitable professionals, and embarking on a cooperative path to improved resilience and well-being.

Understanding the Benefits of Professional Guidance: Specialist support is provided by professional guidance. We'll explore the idea that getting help from experts—like coaches, mentors, counselors, or therapists—offers a special and customized method for dealing with problems and promoting personal development.

Recognizing the Range of Professional Services: Different professions provide different services. We'll go over the many responsibilities of therapists, counselors, coaches, and mentors, assisting people in comprehending the range of each and choosing the right kind of support for their requirements.

Recognizing the Benefits of Professional Guidance

Acknowledgment is the initial phase. We'll go over warning signals and circumstances that can make getting professional help especially helpful, stressing that taking the proactive approach is an investment in one's own growth and well-being.

Dispelling Myths and Stigmas: Dispelling stigmas encourages transparency. We'll talk about typical stigmas and myths about getting professional help, inspiring people to break through social barriers and accept the notion that asking for assistance is a sign of strength.

Selecting the Correct Professional: In business partnerships, compatibility is essential. In order to make sure people find a helpful companion on their trip, we'll go over important aspects to take into account when selecting a professional, such as experience, approach, and personal connection.

Developing rapport and trust: Effective guidance is predicated on trust. We'll go over how to establish rapport and trust with experts in order to create a setting where people feel comfortable, understood, and free to talk about their struggles.

Clearly defining expectations and goals: The process is guided by clarity. We'll talk about how crucial it is to have precise objectives and expectations when working with

8i: Honoring Minor Victories: Developing Drive and Welfare

This chapter delves into the transforming practice of celebrating tiny victories, which is an effective means of promoting resilience, motivation, and general well-being. Come learn how to recognize and value small victories, which can help people develop a positive outlook and advance on their path to personal development.

Recognizing the Importance of Small Wins: Progress is made in major ways through small wins. We'll dive into the knowledge that celebrating and recognizing even the smallest of successes sets off a positive feedback loop that promotes motivation and accelerates the achievement of bigger objectives.

Developing a Growth-Oriented Mentality: This kind of thinking welcome advancement. We'll look at how acknowledging little victories promotes resilience and personal growth by supporting an attitude that sees obstacles as teaching moments.

Acknowledging the Variety of Small Wins: Small victories can take many different shapes. We'll talk about the variety of little triumphs, including those related to relationships, job, well-being, and personal growth, stressing that identifying progress is a subjective and individual process.

Accepting the Process Above Perfection: The trip holds equal significance as the final destination. We'll discuss the idea of choosing the process over perfection, emphasizing how focusing on ongoing, changing growth instead of the final result is achieved by appreciating little victories.

Establishing a Positive Culture: Gratifying little victories makes the atmosphere happier. We'll talk about how people can create an environment that promotes everyone's well-being by recognizing and celebrating their accomplishments and creating a culture of positivity.

Establishing Reasonable Goals: Reasonable goals improve motivation. We'll discuss the significance of establishing realistic objectives and acknowledging small victories to make sure people feel proud of their efforts and stay motivated.

Thinking Back on Personal Development: Developing oneself is an ongoing process. We'll talk about the process of taking stock of one's own development and recognizing the adjustments, growth, and changes that go into a developing sense of self and wellbeing.

Promoting Intrinsic Motivation: Persistent effort is driven by intrinsic motivation. We'll look at how internal motivation, or intrinsic motivation, is fostered by recognizing tiny victories and how it supports perseverance and dedication.

Sharing Success with Others: Joy is increased when wins are shared. We'll talk about the advantages of recognizing and celebrating success with loved ones, coworkers, or friends in order to foster a sense of community and highlight the advantages of personal growth.

Resilience Building Through Acknowledgement: Resilience is increased when successes are acknowledged. We'll look at how acknowledging little accomplishments makes a person more resilient to setbacks and helps them feel capable and flexible when faced with hardship.

Managing Ambition with Self-Compassion: Self-compassion and ambition coexist. We'll talk about the significance of striking a balance between self-compassion and lofty objectives, realizing that appreciating little victories is consistent with a compassionate and understanding attitude to personal growth.

Developing a Customary Celebration Ceremony: Customs heighten the importance of victories. We'll discuss the concept of developing private celebration rituals, which can be straightforward or complex ways to commemorate accomplishments and give them additional significance.

Using Technology to Track Progress: Progress tracking is made easier by technology. We'll talk about how people can document and celebrate little victories using apps, journals, or other tools, which will help them create a visual record of their journey and build a sense of success.

Developing Gratitude for Achievements: Having gratitude increases the significance of victories. We'll talk about the mindfulness practice of expressing gratitude for little wins, focusing on how it can heighten the happiness and positive feelings that come with individual accomplishments.

Keeping Up the Moment with Celebration: People move forward when they celebrate. We'll talk about how keeping momentum going by consistently praising.

Fostering a journey of lifelong well-being

Throughout our trip through the pages of "Practical Tools for Emotional Wellbeing," we have looked at a wide range of approaches, realizations, and routines that support long-term wellbeing. In order to equip people to traverse the intricacies of emotions, relationships, and life's transitions with resilience, mindfulness, and a growth-oriented mentality, a tapestry of useful answers, skills, and resources has been waived.

Thinking Back on the Journey: As we come to the end of our investigation, pause to consider the knowledge obtained, the resources obtained, and the personal development that has occurred. Acknowledge your ability to influence your emotional environment and create a life filled with wellbeing.

Adopting a Holistic Perspective:
The goal of well-being is comprehensive. It entails taking care of the body, mind, and soul. We've discussed techniques for developing self-awareness, realistic approaches to emotional control, and strategies for dealing with conditions like stress, anxiety, sadness, and pain during this journey.

Developing Mindfulness in Everyday Life:
Throughout the journey, mindfulness has emerged as a recurrent topic. The development of mindful awareness has been proposed as a fundamental component for maintaining well-being, whether it is through conscious decision-making, accepting change with fortitude, or engaging in thankfulness practices.

Developing Resilience in the Face of Difficulties:
Difficulties will inevitably arise, but resilience can act as a compass. We've talked about how crucial it is to accept changes, grow from failures, and acknowledge little victories. As a way of thinking and a collection of abilities, resilience enables people to overcome hardship and turn life's unavoidable curveballs around.

Building Connections and Asking for Help: It has been said that having relationships with other people is a source of strength. The significance of relationships and support systems in promoting well-being has been emphasized. This can be achieved by good communication skills, serving as therapists for clients, or seeking expert advice when necessary.

Recognizing the Journey, Step by Step:
It's important to enjoy the journey as we make our way toward wellbeing. Acknowledgment should be given to little victories, personal development, and the persistent pursuit of a growth-oriented mindset. Every action adds to the overall picture of wellbeing.

Promoting Long-Term Well-Being: Promoting long-term well-being is a continuous process rather than a goal. These pages provide tools and insights that are intended to be your guides and allies as you continue to discover, grow, and adjust on your own journey toward long-term well-being.

May this voyage serve as a stimulant for constructive change, promoting a life characterized by emotional equilibrium, self-awareness, and a profound sense of fulfillment. Recall that seeking well-being is a lifetime journey that get better with every deliberate step you take. May the quest of long-lasting well-being provide your courage, resiliency, and happiness as you move through the chapters of your life.sing little victories starts a positive feedback loop that inspires people to keep working hard and making progress.

I hope that the habit of acknowledging little victories will bring you happiness, inspiration, and fortitude as you pursue your goals of wellbeing and personal development.

8j: Adaptability in Change

Transitional Resilience: Handling Change with Fortitude and Flexibility
The fundamental characteristic of resilience in times of transition—a dynamic force that enables people to face change with fortitude, flexibility, and an optimistic outlook—is examined in this chapter. Come learn about the fundamentals of resilience, developing a resilient mentality, and thriving in the face of possibilities and uncertainty brought about by transitions.

Knowing the Code of Resilience: Being resilient is a fundamental strength. We'll explore the idea that resilience is a dynamic process of growing, adapting, and thriving in the face of change and transition rather than just overcoming obstacles.

Accepting Change as an Unavoidable Constant: Life is full of change. We'll look at how accepting change as a necessary and ongoing part of life creates the foundation for resilience development and an open, flexible mentality.

Developing a Resilient Mentality: Resilience is shaped by mindset. We will talk about the significance of developing a resilient mindset, which is an attitude that values adaptation, see obstacles as chances for development, and keep a positive viewpoint when things are changing.

Acknowledging Resources and Strengths: Strength comes from within. We'll look at the process of identifying one's own assets and outside help, stressing that resilience is frequently powered by the capacity to take advantage of one's innate qualities and enlist the aid of others around one.

Developing Adversity Coping Strategies: Coping techniques increase resilience. We'll talk about many coping strategies that people can learn to deal with hardship, such as how to solve problems, control their emotions, and ask for help when the need it.

Building Emotional Resilience: One of the main pillars of strength is emotional resilience. We'll look at techniques for building emotional resilience, which enables people to deal with the emotional parts of change while maintaining their self-awareness, empathy, and ability to recover from failures.

Acquiring Knowledge from Failures and Setbacks: Setbacks serve as stepping stones. We'll talk about the transforming potential of learning from mistakes and setbacks, stressing that building resilience is taking the good things that come from adversity and turning them into opportunities for personal development.

Managing Uncertainty with Grace: Resilience can be fostered by embracing uncertainty. We'll look at techniques for handling uncertainty gracefully, understanding that people's resilience grows when they welcome the unknown with curiosity and a readiness to venture into unexplored ground.

Developing Flexibility in Thought: One of the main components of resilience is flexibility. We'll talk about the value of developing a flexible mindset, which includes being receptive to different viewpoints, modifying objectives, and modifying tactics in response to how transitions change over time.

Getting in Touch with Support Systems: Support networks increase resiliency. We'll discuss the importance of maintaining relationships with friends, family, mentors, or community networks throughout times of change, acknowledging that having a solid support network offers both practical and emotional support.

Preserving Self-Compassion During Change: Self-compassion is a calming energy. We'll talk about practicing self-compassion throughout change, focusing on how important it is to be kind and understanding to oneself, particularly while dealing with difficulties or uncertainty.

Juggling Reflection and Action: Resilient action is informed by reflection. We'll discuss striking a balance between proactive measures to help people thrive and adjust to change and reflective moments where people evaluate their experiences, feelings, and personal development.

Appreciating Minor Victories Along the Way: Minor victories strengthen perseverance. We'll talk about the transforming power of recognizing even the smallest steps toward progress accomplished, maintaining an optimistic outlook, and celebrating tiny victories throughout times of change.

Creating Realistic Transition Goals: Resilience is enhanced by realistic goals. We'll discuss how to develop realistic goals for those going through a transition so they have definite ambitions that complement their values and give them a sense of purpose.

Building a Growth attitude: Resilience is fueled by a growth attitude. We'll talk about how embracing a growth-oriented viewpoint—perceiving obstacles as chances for growth and learning—builds resilience and gives people the ability to flourish during change.

Seeking Expert Advice When Needed: Expert assistance improves resilience. We'll discuss the need of getting advice from mentors, therapists, or counselors when going through a shift, realizing that professional help can offer insightful information and helpful coping mechanisms.

I hope that learning about resilience in transition will help you on your path by giving you the tools you need to handle change with fortitude, flexibility, and a perspective that sees obstacles as chances for development and success.

Chapter 9:Nurturing a Lifelong Journey of Well-Being

Fostering a journey of lifelong well-being Throughout our trip through the pages of "Practical Tools for Emotional Wellbeing," we have looked at a wide range of approaches, realizations, and routines that support long-term wellbeing. In order to equip people to traverse the intricacies of emotions, relationships, and life's transitions with resilience, mindfulness, and a growth-oriented mentality, a tapestry of useful answers, skills, and resources has been waived.

Thinking Back on the Journey: As we come to the end of our investigation, pause to consider the knowledge obtained, the resources obtained, and the personal development that has occurred. Acknowledge your ability to influence your emotional environment and create a life filled with wellbeing.

Adopting a Holistic Perspective:
The goal of well-being is comprehensive. It entails taking care of the body, mind, and soul. We've discussed techniques for developing self-awareness, realistic approaches to emotional control, and strategies for dealing with conditions like stress, anxiety, sadness, and pain during this journey.

Developing Mindfulness in Everyday Life:
Throughout the journey, mindfulness has emerged as a recurrent topic. The development of mindful

awareness has been proposed as a fundamental component for maintaining well-being, whether it is through conscious decision-making, accepting change with fortitude, or engaging in thankfulness practices.

Developing Resilience in the Face of Difficulties: Difficulties will inevitably arise, but resilience can act as a compass. We've talked about how crucial it is to accept changes, grow from failures, and acknowledge little victories. As a way of thinking and a collection of abilities, resilience enables people to overcome hardship and turn life's unavoidable curveballs around.

Building Connections and Asking for Help: It has been said that having relationships with other people is a source of strength. The significance of relationships and support systems in promoting well-being has been emphasized. This can be achieved by good communication skills, serving as therapists for clients, or seeking expert advice when necessary.

Recognizing the Journey, Step by Step:

It's important to enjoy the journey as we make our way toward wellbeing. Acknowledgement should be given to little victories, personal development, and the persistent pursuit of a growth-oriented mindset. Every action adds to the overall picture of wellbeing.

Promoting Long-Term Well-Being: Promoting long-term well-being is a continuous process rather than a goal. These pages provide tools and insights that are intended to be your guides and allies as you continue to discover, grow, and adjust on your own journey toward long-term well-being.

May this voyage serve as a stimulant for constructive change, promoting a life characterized by emotional equilibrium, self-awareness, and a profound sense of fulfillment. Recall that seeking well-being is a lifetime journey that get better with every deliberate step you take. May the quest of long-lasting well-being provide your courage, resiliency, and happiness as you move through the chapters of your life.

Conclusion

An Inspiring End to Your Trip

Upon arriving at the conclusion of "Practical Tools for Emotional Wellbeing," I cordially urge you to pause and reflect on the journey we have undertaken together—a voyage of self-exploration, resiliency, and the quest for enduring well-being.

You have come across a multitude of resources, ideas, and tactics inside the fabric of these pages that are intended to assist you on your journey. This book's heartbeat is a resonance of your own fortitude, resiliency, and potential for development.

You are an explorer, not just a reader, one who is exploring the unknown waters of change, scaling the summits of self-awareness, and mapping the regions of your emotions. Your path is distinct, and in these words you have found support, direction, and, hopefully, a bit of motivation.

Recall that achieving well-being is a dynamic, lifetime journey rather than a destination. Every tool you have found is a lantern, shedding light on the way forward. Little victories celebrate your development and serve as lighthouses. Failures are stepping stones rather than obstacles, and resilience is the strong boat that gets you through life's changes.

Take the strength of resilience, the power of mindfulness, and the knowledge you have received from each chapter with you when you leave these pages. Accept change as a chance, make conscious choices, and acknowledge and appreciate all of your accomplishments, no matter how minor.

You have the potential to be happy for a very long time. You are still writing new chapters in the story of your life with each breath. Take a bold step toward the unknown, move to the best of change, and revel in the wonder of your own development.

This book is only one chapter in the long story of your life; you are welcome to continue exploring with the knowledge and skills you have gained along the way. Your well-being is a huge canvas, and you are the artist creating the work of art that is your own life.

Thus, my beloved explorer, may your path be filled with self-realization, fortitude, and a steadfast dedication to your health. May the next chapter of your life, which you turn to, be one that is full of fulfillment, purpose, and the resonance of your own brave heart.

Review

Dear Reader

I hope this message finds you well. As the author of Practical Tool For Emotional Well-being, I am reaching out to express my sincere gratitude for choosing to embark on the journey of emotional well-being with me.

Your insights are invaluable, and I would love to hear your thoughts on the book. Whether it's a brief comment or a more detailed review, your feedback contributes to the ongoing dialogue around mental health and well-being.

Here are a few prompts to guide your review:

What resonated with you the most in the book? Were here specific tools or insights that you found particularly helpful?

How has the book influenced your approach to emotional well-being?

Your honest feedback not only helps me as an author but also provides potential readers with valuable insights. If you could take a moment to share your thoughts on [platforms where the book is available, e.g., Amazon], it would mean a great deal.

Thank you for being part of this journey. Your voice matters, and I appreciate your time and consideration.

Wishing you continued growth and well-being,
Dr. Sherrie R. Salls, PhD
Author, Practical Tools for Emotional Well-being

www.ingramcontent.com/pod-product-compliance
Lightning Source LLC
Chambersburg PA
CBHW070921260726

48661CB00003B/775